MARKS & SPENCER

A GUIDE TO
WILD
[illegible]S

JOHN AKEROYD

First Collins edition published 1996

Revised edition published 2004

This edition published 2007 for Marks & Spencer plc

www.marksandspencer.com

ISBN-10: 0-00-778061-3
ISBN-13: 978-0-00-778061-7

07 08 09 10
1 2 3 4 5 6 7 8 9 10

Printed and bound in Hong Kong

INTRODUCTION

This book introduces 240 of the commoner wild flowers of Britain and Ireland. These are the wild plants, both native and introduced, that we see around us and encounter on a walk in the countryside, suburb or even, mostly as weeds, in the town. (Weeds are opportunist plants that colonise ground modified by human activity and disturbance.)

Britain and Ireland have more than 1,500 wild flowers (including grasses, sedges and rushes). This is a relatively small number on a world scale, but their recognition presents a formidable task for the beginner. The selection of species to include here has not been easy. I have tried to include those wild flowers that are likely to be encountered in the lowlands. In a book of this sort it is not possible to describe and illustrate all of, for example, the forget-me-nots, speedwells or water buttercups, but at least this book will make you aware that they exist as a group. Any apparent bias towards southern England, reflects as much as anything a richer lowland flora here through the influence of complex historical and climatic factors.

Ireland is often given a mention in its own right as too many people in Britain, not just botanists, forget that it is a separate geographical entity, with its own climate and flora. The book does not cover the special wild flowers of highland Britain and Ireland, which need their own volume, or the grasses, sedges and rushes. The ferns and their allies are excluded because they do not have flowers.

Our flora is constantly changing and even my lifetime has seen much destruction, especially of the traditionally managed meadows that were once bright with wild flowers. The flora is also being modified, and often enriched, by new arrivals and the spread of more established plants. That is why I have included such denizens as Canadian Fleabane and Gallant Soldier alongside the more familiar and well-loved Daffodil, Primrose and Violet. May we learn to love each of them, for they all have their place and collectively they represent Britain and Ireland's most fragile and precious heritage and natural resource.

HOW TO USE THIS BOOK

This book describes the key features of our commoner wild flowers and is a guide to their identification. Each plant has a page to itself, illustrated by a **colour photograph** that can be compared with the plant in the field. The photograph may show either details of the flowers or fruits, or the general habit; many wild flowers can be recognised even at a distance by a striking or characteristic appearance. A **silhouette** at the top of the page gives a thumbnail sketch of the shape and colour of the flower or flower cluster.

Plants are grouped by family, but bear in mind that some, such as the Rose and the Figwort families, display a range of flower structures that can confuse even the experienced botanist! A shaded **calendar bar** shows those months in which each species is most likely to flower. Some wild flowers, like the orchids, have a short, precise flowering period. Others, like Red Campion, have a distinct flowering season but may be found in flower at almost any time. Some annual weeds, such as Chickweed and Groundsel, flower throughout the year except during severe frost and snow.

The **main text** describes the general habit of each plant and some key facts about its ecology and distribution. Details of distribution are included only where a species is not found more or less throughout Britain and Ireland. Other notes are included on such topics as pollinators and predators, seed dispersal, uses by people for food or medicine, and interesting facts or folklore. All plants have a story to tell.

Key features for checking identification are set out in the **ID Fact File**. This section includes 'Lookalikes', which compares similar plants on other pages or briefly describes other, often rarer, plants that are not given full entries in the text. Some of these may in fact be common in localised areas.

A **map** shows the distribution of each plant in western Europe. It indicates parts of Britain and Ireland from which the plant is absent and often shows how some plants reach the edge of their range here. Plant distributions are fascinating. Some plants have a very western distribution in Europe, for example Gorse; others a more southern or northern one.

LOOKING FOR WILD FLOWERS

Wild flowers are all around us. They live in the fragments of natural habitat that remain, and in the fields, waysides and hedgerows created and moulded over centuries of human activity; they are even present in the apparently devastated wastelands of our suburbs and inner cities. Not all are natives, for many, perhaps a majority, have come in from abroad to become as familiar as the real natives; in most cases we will never know their true status. Most have a history of human use for food, drugs or craft and building materials. Some have only very recently arrived, but are spreading happily in our post-intensive agricultural and post-industrial landscape.

So where is it best to look for wild flowers? The answer is that they are everywhere, but they sometimes need to be sought out or hunted down. For a few, a trip is needed to certain special places, like the wild limestone hills of the Burren region of County Clare, the coastal heaths of Cornwall or the sandy commons of the Breckland of East Anglia; a visit to the chalk grassland of southern England and the surviving ancient woodlands to see some of our best diversity of wild plant life is essential. The late Oleg Polunin, one of Europe's greatest field botanists who had seen plants all around the world, recommended the seaside cliffs and sand-dunes of western Britain and Ireland above all as places to see displays of colourful and interesting wild flowers.

A few ground rules will give the observer a good selection of species. Seek out rivers, lakes and other wetlands; explore commons and heathlands; look on broken, rocky ground, especially near the sea – sand-dunes are always good – and so on. These habitats are often the last fragments of a richer landscape, relics of an era before today's intensive land use. Nevertheless, a walk around a village or town, a glance at any open space, copse or streamside in suburbia, or a few hedges and woods and arable fields in the countryside, will provide a rich variety of plants. Wild flowers are an integral part of the landscape scene, lending colour, atmosphere or even, like the tall teasels and mulleins, structural variety to the view from the rambler's path, or that from the moving car or train.

IDENTIFICATION OF WILD FLOWERS

Many people are put off plants and botany by the apparent difficulty in sorting out the great range of forms and structures of flowers. This book avoids using specialist terminology, some of which is mere jargon, but it is important to employ certain terms for clarity. These terms may seem outlandish, if only because they derive from Latin and Greek, for centuries the universal languages of botany. Scientific names of plants are themselves Latin words, and botanists still introduce a new species in the form of a published Latin description, a useful international convention. Botanists use a range of descriptive terms, derived from Latin, to denote the shapes of leaves and other parts.

Plants vary in their life histories. An **annual** grows, flowers, sets seed and dies within a single season or year. Other plants that live longer are **biennials**, which form an overwintering plant in one year and flower in the next, and **perennials**, which grow and flower over several years. The roots of perennials are often modified as storage structures to enable them to survive the winter and put on new growth in the spring. Some, with **bulbs**, fleshy underground shoots, die back during the summer; they thus avoid either dry periods or the summer shade of woodland. A common structure is a fleshy, creeping root, the **rhizome**. This not only stores food, but propagates the plant vegetatively without the need for seeds.

Flowers and the number and arrangement of their various parts or organs provide the most important characters used to classify the flowering plants. The structure of the **flower** is shown in Figures 1 & 2. Each flower is a special shoot, with successive whorls of parts that probably represent modified leaves. Sometimes the flower is associated with or surrounded by special leaves, the **bracts**. The flowers of the daisy and dandelion family are tiny (florets) and massed in heads. The lowest and outermost whorl or layer of the flower itself is made up of **sepals** (collectively known as the **calyx**) that enclose and protect the flower when it is in bud. Sepals are usually green or dully coloured. The next whorl is the petals (collectively known as the **corolla**), usually but by no means always, brightly coloured. The petals are what catch the eye of the observer

– and that of the visiting insect. Where petals and sepals are not clearly differentiated they are referred to as the **perianth**.

Within these two whorls lie the reproductive parts, male and female. The male parts are the **stamens**, stalked structures that contain pollen within bag-like anthers. The coloured, dust-like pollen, usually transferred by insects or wind, fertilises minute **ovules** (within each of which is an egg cell) contained inside the female structure or **ovary**. The ovary comprises one or more **carpels**, which contain the ovules; each carpel bears a pointed, knobbly or feathery **stigma** to trap the pollen. The stigma is often on a stalk or **style**.

After a carpel has been fertilised, it develops into a fruit, containing one to many **seeds**. Each one is a neatly packaged embryonic plant, protected by a hard coat and containing a supply of food, usually starch, either in the seed-leaves themselves or as a separate foodstore.

Fruits are classified into a number of categories: a common one is the **capsule**, a dry fruit that splits to release the seeds. A **berry** is a many-seeded, fleshy fruit; a **drupe** or **drupelet** is a one-seeded, fleshy fruit. A **nut** or **nutlet** is a one-seeded, dry fruit.

Half flowers showing structure

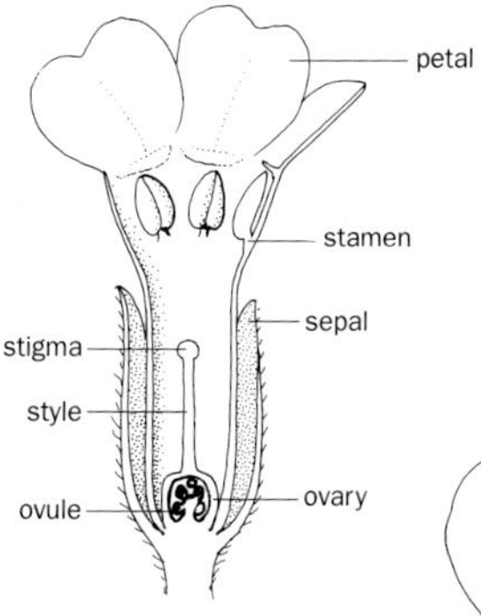

Figure 1 Cowslip.

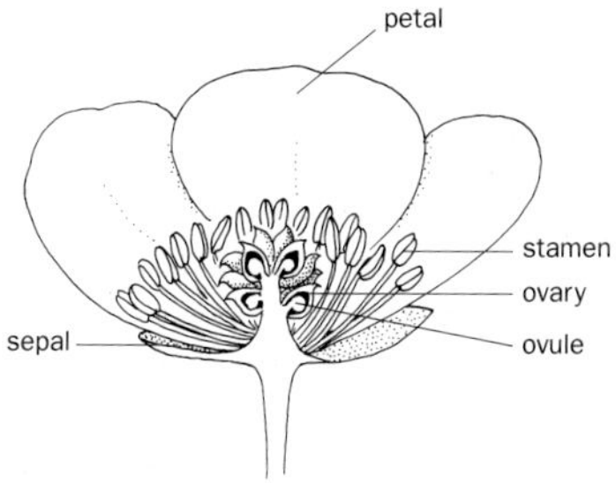

Figure 2 Buttercup.

THE HABITATS OF WILD FLOWERS

Vegetation, the complex communities in which plants grow in close association with one another, lies beyond the scope of this book. However, it needs a brief introduction, since particular habitats are mentioned in the text.

After the glaciers had retreated from Britain and Ireland at the end of the last Ice Age, some 10,000 years ago, the landscape was one of open tundra not unlike what we see today in Arctic regions. Fragments also survive in the highlands, especially in Scotland. Other plants gradually recolonised the lowlands, especially those that favoured open and wet ground. In time, woodland and, in wetter western areas, peat bogs came to cover the landscape, restricting the plants of open habitats to cliffs, mountains, river banks, and coastal shingle beaches and sand-dunes.

As human activity opened up the landscape from the latter part of the Stone Age, opportunist plants that we know today as weeds moved into the newly disturbed habitats, especially land cleared for cultivation. Other plants that had been displaced by woodland colonised grasslands and heaths, kept open by cutting, burning and grazing of stock. In parts of western and northern Britain and Ireland, peat invaded areas where woodland had been cleared by early farmers. All over, the woodlands shrunk and are today represented by the so-called 'ancient woodlands' managed since even before the Middle Ages for the production of timber, brushwood, charcoal and game. Wetlands were drained, rivers were canalised and coastal defences modified the form of sand-dunes and saltmarshes. In the present century, public and commercial forestry and intensive agriculture have further altered the landscape and its vegetation and flora. In recent years there has been a trend for scrub to invade grassland and existing scrub to develop into woodland.

What we see in the British Isles at the end of the 20th century is one of the world's most modified landscapes, but one that is still surprisingly rich in plant life. Our mosaic of natural and semi-natural vegetation vividly represents all facets of the history of plant and animal life and human society since the end of the Ice Age.

CONSERVATION

Our precious heritage of wild flowers is under constant threat from all sides. The main problem is one of pressure of land use and the destruction, degradation, fragmentation and isolation of habitats. Modern, intensive agriculture has transformed a varied landscape into huge prairies and monocultures, often without hedges or any marginal land. Industry and housing are greedy to take over great tracts of land. New roads will continue to cut through sites rich in plant and animal life. There may even be a long-term threat from climate change. Already this century we have lost many wetland plants from southern England, as water use has risen and drought has increased.

Individuals, too, are often blamed, and it is true that the Victorian naturalists frequently overdid their enthusiasm to collect rarities. However, habitat destruction is the real villain. Contrary to popular belief, it has never been illegal to pick most wild flowers. Nevertheless, the maxim 'leave wild flowers for others to enjoy' is a useful guide. The modern countryside has fewer reserves of plants to buffer any further loss or removal. What *is* certainly true is that, under the terms of the Wildlife and Countryside Act 1981, *it is illegal to dig up plants without the permission of the owner of the land on which they grow.* The Act also gives full protection from picking or uprooting to a group of plants that are so rare and threatened that they could disappear unless so earmarked. Of the species included in the present book, only Fritillary is so protected in Britain.

In the Republic of Ireland, plants are protected under the Flora Protection Order (1987), which protects the habitat of 68 threatened species. The only species included in this book that is covered by the Order is Betony, one of several widespread plants that have a curiously rare or local distribution in Ireland. Bee Orchid, Betony, Cowslip and Moschatel are protected in Northern Ireland under the Wildlife (NI) Order (1985).

It is the sincere hope of many botanists that one day we shall see flowers return to our countryside in enough numbers for anybody to pick them, sparingly and sensibly, without having to worry at all about their survival.

WHAT NEXT?

Readers who would like to take their studies of wild flowers further, and perhaps meet others with a similar interest, are recommended to contact any of the following organisations concerned with the study and conservation of wild plants. These organisations publish newsletters or magazines, with articles on wild flowers. There are also numerous local natural history societies and field clubs throughout Britain and Ireland.

The Botanical Society of the British Isles, c/o Natural History Museum, Cromwell Road, London SW7 5BD, is for amateur and professional botanists; members record and make studies of the wild flowers and ferns of Britain and Ireland.
Plantlife, 14 Rollestone Street, Salisbury SP1 1DX, promotes a wider public interest in the wild plants of Britain and other countries, and campaigns to protect them and their habitats.
The Wild Flower Society, 68 Outwoods Road, Loughborough, Leicestershire LE11 3LY, encourages a love of British and Irish wild flowers, especially amongst young people, through plant hunting and recording.
The Royal Society for Nature Conservation, The Green, Witham Park, Lincoln LN5 7JR, co-ordinates a national network of County Naturalists and Wildlife Trusts throughout Britain and Northern Ireland.
The Irish Biogeographical Society, c/o Natural History Museum, Kildare Street, Dublin 2, studies the distribution of plants and animals in Ireland.

J	F	M	A	M	J
J	A	S	O	N	D

Hop
Humulus lupulus

Rough-hairy perennial, twining and trailing on hedges, shrubs, trees or wire-netting fences; cultivated in SE England and the Vale of Evesham, but often naturalised, and sometimes truly wild in damp woods. It is widespread in Britain, but rare in Scotland and Ireland, where it is introduced. The dried fruiting heads have been used in Britain since the late Middle Ages to flavour and preserve beer; also, in pillows, to aid sleep. The young shoots can be cooked as a green vegetable.

ID FACT FILE

Height: 3–6 m

Flowers: In greenish, hanging clusters, the male branched, the female cone-like with pale green bracts, each on separate plants

Leaves: In opposite pairs, up to 10 cm long, heart-shaped, 3- to 5-lobed, coarsely toothed

Fruits: Cone-like, hanging heads, about 3 cm long

Lookalikes: Hemp (*Cannabis sativa*) is an erect, often branched annual 1–3 m tall, the leaves compound, with 6–9 segments, of waste ground and tips, but increasingly cultivated for fibre.

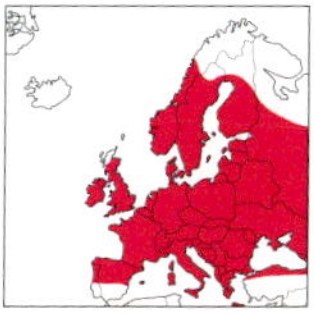

J	F	M	A	M	J
J	A	S	O	N	D

Stinging Nettle

Urtica dioica

ID FACT FILE

HEIGHT: 50–150 cm, sometimes up to 250 cm

FLOWERS: Tiny, in greenish, hanging, tassel-like clusters, the male and female on separate plants

LEAVES: In opposite pairs, up to 10 cm long, heart- or spear-shaped, pointed, regularly toothed

FRUITS: 1–1.5 mm across, each enclosing a single seed

LOOKALIKES: Annual Nettle (*Urtica urens*) is a smaller, often branched annual up to 60 cm tall, of cultivated land or light soils.

Erect, unbranched perennial, usually covered with long stinging hairs; it has square stems, arising from tough, yellow roots and creeping underground stems, and forms large patches. Abundant on waysides and waste ground, around buildings, in gardens, ditches, marshes and damp woods, especially places where the soil is enriched by animal manure or fertilizer. The stems are an ancient source of fibre and the shoots provide a green vegetable. Caterpillars of several butterflies feed on the leaves.

J	F	M	A	M	J
J	A	S	O	N	D

Redshank or Persicaria

Persicaria maculosa

ID FACT FILE

Height: 10–80 cm

Flowers: Pale or bright pink, massed in dense, cylindrical spikes 1–3 cm long

Leaves: Narrow, spear-shaped, pointed, often with a dark blotch

Fruits: 2–3 mm long, triangular or lens-shaped, black, shiny

Lookalikes: Pale Persicaria (*Persicaria lapathifolia*) has greenish-white or dull pink flowers and flower-stalks covered with tiny, rough, yellowish hairs.

More or less hairless, erect or sometimes sprawling, branched annual. Common on cultivated land; also on bare mud and gravel beside streams, rivers and lakes. One of the most persistent weeds of farmland, sometimes colouring crops pink where it has escaped the farmer's spray, and a common plant of gardens and disturbed, waste places. Plants from waterside habitats are often smaller and little-branched. The starch-rich fruits were formerly gathered and used as a grain.

J	F	M	A	M	J
J	A	S	O	N	D

Amphibious Bistort

Persicaria amphibia

ID FACT FILE

Height: 10–100 cm

Flowers: Deep pink, massed in dense, stout, cylindrical spikes on long stems

Leaves: Floating leaves spear-shaped, blunt, hairless; leaves of land plants pointed, minutely hairy

Fruits: Lens-shaped, 2–3 mm long, brown, shiny

Lookalikes: On land may be confused with Redshank or Pale Persicaria (p.13). Bistort (*Persicaria bistorta*), with narrowly triangular leaves, forms clumps in damp grassland in N Britain and locally elsewhere.

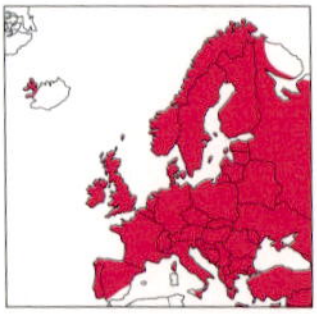

Usually aquatic, little-branched perennial, with floating stems and leaves, widespread in lakes, ponds, canals and flooded ditches. Its creeping roots spread to form large patches that can create a conspicuous and attractive pink band around the margins of still or slow-moving bodies of water. This species also grows on land, sometimes as a weed of cultivation, where the plants are erect, have narrow, rather hairy leaves and produce fewer, scruffier heads of flowers.

J	F	M	A	M	J
J	A	S	O	N	D

Black Bindweed

Fallopia convolvulus

ID FACT FILE

HEIGHT: 10–120 cm

FLOWERS: Inconspicuous, greenish-white or greenish-pink in small clusters or loose spikes

LEAVES: Heart- or arrow-shaped, pointed

FRUITS: Matt black, triangular nuts up to 5 mm long, each enclosed in papery remains of perianth

LOOKALIKES: Field Bindweed (p.142) and Hedge Bindweed (p.143) are unrelated twining plants with white or pink, trumpet-shaped flowers.

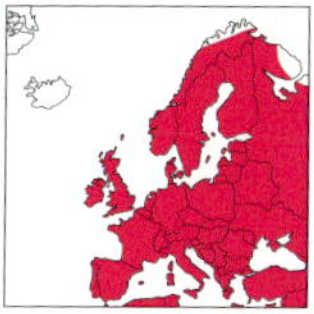

Annual, prostrate or twining plant of cultivated land. Archaeological sites reveal that it has long been a weed of cultivation in Britain, and its fruits were until recently a major contaminant of agricultural seed. It represents a significant proportion of the seed bank of cultivated land. Plants sometimes have winged perianths, especially on rich soil, which are similar to those of the rarer Copse Bindweed (*Fallopia dumetorum*), of woodland margins and hedgerows.

J	F	M	A	M	J
J	A	S	O	N	D

Japanese Knotweed

Fallopia japonica

ID FACT FILE

Height: 100–250 cm

Flowers: Greenish-white, sometimes pink, in branched clusters

Leaves: Heart-shaped, abruptly cut off at the base, pointed, rather stiff

Fruits: Rarely formed in Britain and Ireland

Lookalikes: The less widespread Giant Knotweed (*Fallopia sachalinense*) is even larger, up to 4 m tall, with more oblong leaves, heart-shaped at the base.

Robust, hairless perennial, with vigorous rhizomes and stout, hollow, reddish stems, arching and branched in the upper part. Forming dense thickets on waste ground, derelict land, railway embankments and cuttings, road-verges and untended gardens. Originally from Japan, this plant is perhaps the worst weed ever to have reached Britain and Ireland, where it is spreading rapidly. The Wildlife and Countryside Act 1981 forbids its deliberate introduction into the wild in Britain.

J	F	M	A	M	J
J	A	S	O	N	D

Sorrel

Rumex acetosa

ID FACT FILE

HEIGHT: 10–120 cm

FLOWERS: Minute, reddish or greenish, in branched spikes, the male and female on separate plants

LEAVES: Basal and lower stem leaves stalked, spear- to arrow-shaped, blunt, with a pair of downward-pointing lobes at the base; upper leaves stalkless

FRUITS: 3-sided shiny brown nuts, 2–2.5 mm long, each enclosed in brown, papery remains of perianth

LOOKALIKES: Sheep's Sorrel (p.18) is smaller and the basal lobes of the leaves point outwards.

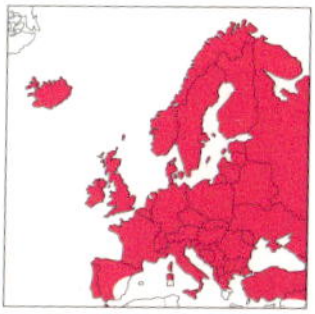

Erect perennial of grassland, road-verges, woodland rides, sand-dunes and rocky ground; it can give a reddish tint to meadows in May and June. The flowers are pollinated by the wind. The whole plant tastes of acid and the leaves can be used in salads or to flavour sauces and soups – although the true Garden Sorrel is a different species. Plants from sand-dune grassland (machair) in Scotland and western Ireland are shorter, less branched and have short white hairs on the stems and leaves.

J	F	M	A	M	J
J	A	S	O	N	D

Sheep's Sorrel

Rumex acetosella

ID FACT FILE

Height: 5–30 cm, sometimes up to 50 cm

Flowers: Minute, reddish, in branched spikes, the male and female on separate plants

Leaves: Narrow, spear-shaped, with a pair of outward-pointing lobes at the base, often reddish

Fruits: 3-sided nuts, 1–1.5 mm long, each enclosed in brown, papery remains of perianth

Lookalikes: Sorrel (p.17) is larger and the basal lobes of the leaves point downwards rather than outwards.

Erect perennial, branched above, with creeping roots, forming sometimes quite extensive patches on heathland, dry grassland, rock outcrops, wall-tops, shingle beaches and sand-dunes on nutrient-poor acid soils. On sandy or peaty soils this plant can be a persistent garden and agricultural weed. The whole plant tastes of acid. The flowers are pollinated by the wind. A very variable species: particularly distinctive are plants from dry heathland, which have very narrow, strap-like leaves.

J	F	M	A	M	J
J	A	S	O	N	D

Broad-leaved Dock

Rumex obtusifolius

ID FACT FILE

Height: 50–150 cm

Flowers: Tiny, green or reddish, in large, loose, leafy spikes

Leaves: Broad, oblong, heart-shaped at base, blunt

Fruits: Tiny triangular nuts, each enclosed in brown, papery perianth, with spiny margins and a single (rarely 3) corky wart

Lookalikes: Other docks; Curled Dock (p.20) has spear-shaped, pointed leaves with curly margins and no spines on the fruit; it rarely forms large clumps.

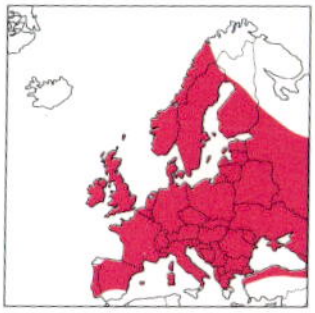

Robust perennial, arising from a stout root and forming conspicuous leafy clumps on cultivated land, waste places and riverbanks. It was, before modern weed-killers, a major weed of cultivation and is listed as noxious under the Weeds Act 1959. It often crosses with Curled Dock (p.20) when the two grow together. The large leaves were used to wrap butter and are said to relieve nettle stings. The flowers are pollinated by the wind, but sometimes by bumblebees.

J	F	M	A	M	J
J	A	S	O	N	D

Curled Dock

Rumex crispus

ID FACT FILE

Height: 50–120 cm, rarely up to 250 cm

Flowers: Tiny, green or somewhat reddish, massed in large, branched spikes

Leaves: Spear-shaped, pointed, with wavy margins

Fruits: Tiny triangular nuts, each enclosed in brown, papery perianth, with untoothed margins and 1–3 corky warts

Lookalikes: Other docks; Broad-leaved Dock (p.19) has broader, blunt leaves without wavy margins and toothed fruits.

Erect perennial, arising from a long root; a widespread plant of cultivated and waste ground, shingle beaches, sand-dunes and tidal mud of estuaries. The seeds are produced in huge numbers and can survive for more than 50 years in soil. It was, before modern weed-killers, a major weed of cultivation and is listed as noxious under the Weeds Act 1959. The flowers are pollinated by the wind, but sometimes by bumblebees. A very variable species, with distinct subspecies on seashores and tidal mud.

J	F	M	A	M	J
J	A	S	O	N	D

Sea Beet

Beta vulgaris

ID FACT FILE

Height: 30–100 cm

Flowers: Green, 3–4 mm in long dense, leafy spikes

Leaves: Triangular, dark green, glossy, leathery, with wavy margins

Fruits: Spherical, 3–4 mm across, enclosed in corky, persistent perianth

Lookalikes: Fat Hen (p.22) is an erect annual of cultivated and waste land that has paler, often floury leaves.

Erect or sprawling, untidy, fleshy perennial, forming prominent clumps on shingle beaches, edges of saltmarshes, sea-walls and coastal rocks and cliffs. It occurs all around British and Irish coasts, except those of N Scotland. The stout root is rich in sugar; indeed, the cultivated sugar beet is a variant of this plant, as are the beetroot, spinach beet and Swiss chard of the garden. The corky fruiting structure allows the seeds to float and to be dispersed along the coast by the tide.

J	F	M	A	M	J
J	A	S	O	N	D

Fat Hen

Chenopodium album

ID FACT FILE

Height: 20–150 cm

Flowers: Tiny, green, massed in many dense, branched clusters

Leaves: Oval, diamond- or paddle-shaped, greyish-green, floury, almost untoothed or coarsely toothed

Fruits: Numerous, tiny, each containing 1 black or brown, flattened, glossy seed

Lookalikes: Sea Beet (p.21) is perennial and has dark green, glossy leaves. Red Goosefoot (*Chenopodium rubrum*), with jagged-toothed leaves, grows around manure heaps and on saltmarshes.

Erect, often robust and spreading branched annual of waste ground and cultivated land, especially on rich soil. This is the commonest of the dozen or so goosefoots – several of them probably introduced – in Britain and Ireland, all plants of disturbed or open ground. Fat Hen was once a valued substitute for spinach and the seeds were eaten as a grain. It is a plant that apparently has no natural habitat and probably evolved alongside human habitation. A very variable species.

J	F	M	A	M	J
J	A	S	O	N	D

Common Orache

Atriplex patula

ID FACT FILE

Height: 20–100 cm

Flowers: Tiny, green, in slender, elongate, dense clusters

Leaves: Triangular or spear-shaped, variably toothed, with a pair of large, forward-pointing teeth near base

Fruits: Many, small, each containing 1 flattened seed, enclosed within triangular, fleshy bracts

Lookalikes: Halberd-leaved Orache (*Atriplex hastata*), a variable, often prostrate plant of cultivated land and seashores, has leaves with the basal teeth spreading at a right angle.

Erect or sprawling, often floury, branched, leafy annual of waste ground and cultivated land, especially on rich soil. This scruffy and undistinguished plant is the commonest of the half-dozen or so oraches native to Britain and Ireland, all of them plants of seashores, saltmarshes or open and disturbed ground. It is a plant that, like Fat Hen (p.22), apparently has no natural habitat and probably evolved alongside human habitation. Oraches, too, have been cooked and eaten like spinach.

J	F	M	A	M	J
J	A	S	O	N	D

Greater Stitchwort

Stellaria holostea

ID FACT FILE

Height: 20–60 cm

Flowers: In loose clusters, white, 15–25 mm across, the 5 petals divided to half-way; 10 pale yellow stamens

Leaves: In opposite pairs, somewhat greyish-green, narrow, rough-margined, tapered from the base to a point

Fruits: Spherical capsules 6–8 mm long, splitting into 6 segments

Lookalikes: Lesser Stitchwort (*Stellaria graminea*) is more slender and straggling, with smaller petals divided to the base. There are a number of similar related species.

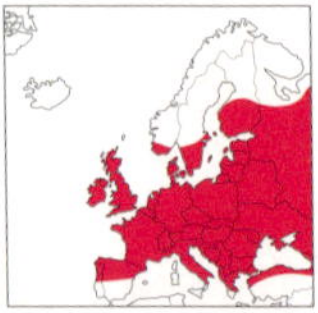

Slender perennial, with weak, brittle, 4-angled stems, forming patches in hedgerows and woodland rides and margins. One of the most characteristic and attractive flowers of spring, brightening waysides with its masses of flowers. Although widespread, it is local in N Scotland and W Ireland and does not occur on the most acid soils. The common name refers to the slender, thread-like flower stalks, or is perhaps an allusion to its use as a folk remedy for a stitch or sudden pain.

J	F	M	A	M	J
J	A	S	O	N	D

All through mild winters.

Chickweed

Stellaria media

ID FACT FILE

Height: 5–40 cm

Flowers: White, 3–10 mm across, with 5 deeply notched petals and 3–8 reddish stamens

Leaves: In opposite pairs, oval or spear-shaped, stalked, 1-veined, pointed

Fruits: Egg-shaped capsules, splitting into 6, drooping when ripe

Lookalikes: Three-nerved Sandwort (*Moehringia trinervia*) has 3–5 veins on each leaf and grows in woodland. Thyme-leaved Sandwort (*Arenaria serpyllifolia*), with tiny stalkless leaves and erect fruits, grows on bare, dry ground.

Prostrate or sprawling annual, with weak, straggling stems marked on opposite sides by a line of hairs. It forms large patches on open ground, especially cultivated land. The plant requires and tolerates high nutrient levels and survives even around manure heaps and seabird nesting cliffs. Chickweed may be a pestilential weed, but is a cheering sight as one of the first flowers of late winter and early spring, along with Shepherd's Purse (p.47), Red Dead-nettle (p.154) and Groundsel (p.215).

J	F	M	A	M	J
J	A	S	O	N	D

Ragged Robin

Lychnis flos-cuculi

ID FACT FILE

Height: 25–90 cm

Flowers: Deep pink, rarely white, 20–25 mm across, each of the 5 petals deeply cut into 4 lobes; calyx 10-veined

Leaves: In opposite pairs, the lower oblong, the upper narrow, spear-shaped, pointed

Fruits: Cylindrical capsules opening by 5 short teeth, each enclosed within persistent, red-veined calyx

Lookalikes: Red Campion (p.27) has shallowly 2-lobed petals and 10 backward-curved capsule-teeth.

Erect, often reddish, branched perennial of marshes, damp meadows, wet woodland clearings and rides, instantly recognisable by the ragged appearance of the pink flowers. It is much less common than formerly because of the destruction of old meadows by modern agriculture, but is increasingly popular in gardens, reflecting John Gerard's comment in his 1597 *Herball*: 'These are not used either in medicine or in nourishment: but they serve for garlands or crowns, and to decke up gardens.'

J	F	M	A	M	J
J	A	S	O	N	D

All through mild winters.

Red Campion

Silene dioica

Hairy, erect, branched biennial or perennial of woodland, shady lanes, hedgerows and coastal cliffs. It is generally common, but scarce in Ireland and local in East Anglia. Often crossing with White Campion (p.28), especially where the habitat has been disturbed. Red Campion is a native woodland plant that has expanded its range perhaps because of adaptation to more open habitats, conferred by generations of such crossing. A handsome double-flowered variant is grown in gardens.

ID FACT FILE

HEIGHT: 20–90 cm

FLOWERS: Deep pink, 15–25 mm across, male and female on separate plants, not scented, with 5 deeply notched petals; calyx 10-veined (male) or 20-veined (female)

LEAVES: In opposite pairs, broadly spear-shaped, pointed, persisting in winter

FRUITS: Cylindrical capsules, opening by 10 curved-back teeth

LOOKALIKES: Similar but taller plants with pale pink flowers are hybrids with White Campion (p.28). Ragged Robin (p.26) has deeply 4-lobed petals.

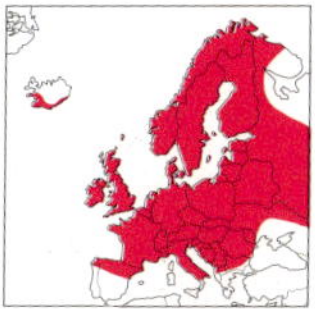

J	F	M	A	M	J
J	A	S	O	N	D

White Campion

Silene latifolia

ID FACT FILE

Height: 30–100 cm

Flowers: White, scented, 20–30 mm across, with 5 deeply notched petals; male and female on separate plants

Leaves: In opposite pairs, broadly spear-shaped, pointed

Fruits: Egg-shaped capsules, 12–18 mm long, opening by 10 erect teeth

Lookalikes: Bladder Campion (p.29) has more inflated, bladder-like calyx and greyish leaves.

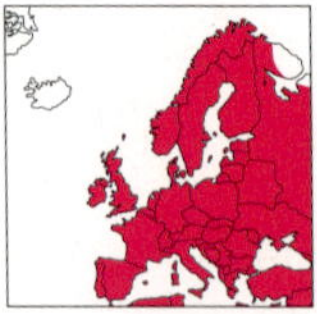

Softly and densely hairy, erect, much-branched biennial, or short-lived perennial, of cultivated land, waysides and hedgerows. Often crossing with Red Campion (p.27), especially where the habitat has been disturbed, giving rise to an array of flower colours. The flowers are most conspicuous and scented at dusk to attract the moths that pollinate them. It is an ancient introduction from S Europe, probably arriving with Stone Age immigrants. It is much less frequent in Ireland and W Scotland.

J	F	M	A	M	J
J	A	S	O	N	D

Bladder Campion

Silene vulgaris

ID FACT FILE

Height: 20–60 cm

Flowers: In loose clusters, white, 10–18 mm across, with 5 deeply notched petals; calyx egg-shaped, bladder-like, yellowish or purplish

Leaves: Oval, rather stiff, pointed, waxy, greyish

Fruits: Cylindrical capsules, opening by 5 teeth, enclosed within persistent papery calyx

Lookalikes: Sea Campion (p.30) is more or less prostrate and has unbranched stems and larger flowers.

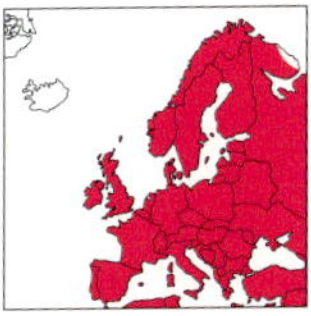

A more or less hairless, greyish, ascending, branched perennial of open grassland, dry banks and cultivated ground. It is generally widespread, if rather local, although rare over much of Scotland, especially the west. A very variable species, which some botanists (and thus wild flower books) do not distinguish from Sea Campion (p.30). The flowers, like those of the more showy White Campion (p.28), are most conspicuous at dusk and are pollinated by night-flying moths.

J	F	M	A	M	J
J	A	S	O	N	D

A few flowers until October.

Sea Campion

Silene uniflora

ID FACT FILE

HEIGHT: 10–30 cm

FLOWERS: Mostly solitary, white, 20–25 mm across, with 5 deeply notched petals; bladder-like calyx cylindrical, greenish, yellowish or purplish

LEAVES: Spear-shaped, stiff, pointed, fleshy, grey

FRUITS: Cylindrical capsules, opening by 5 teeth, enclosed within persistent, papery calyx

LOOKALIKES: Bladder Campion (p.29) is more erect and has branched stems.

Perennial, forming patches and loose cushions on shingle beaches, cliffs, rocks and walls near the sea. It occurs locally inland on mountains, lead-rich rocks, spoil-heaps from lead mines, and on the shores of lakes. In W Wales it sometimes grows in churchyards where chippings of lead-rich rock have been used to cover graves. It is a very variable species, especially in the mountains of W and C Europe, that can be difficult to tell apart from Bladder Campion (p.29).

J	F	M	A	M	J
J	A	S	O	N	D

White Water-lily

Nymphaea alba

ID FACT FILE

Height: 1–2 m

Flowers: White, scented, 10–20 cm across, with 15–25 petals, 4 green sepals and many large, rich yellow stamens

Leaves: Floating, circular, green, up to 30 cm across, rather leathery

Fruits: Large spongy, warty capsules with many seeds

Lookalikes: Ornamental water-lilies, many of them garden hybrids.

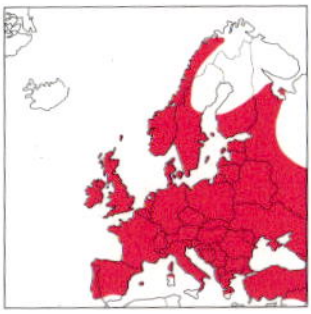

A hairless, aquatic perennial of lakes and other still waters, arising from a massive corky rhizome and sometimes forming large patches. The leaves and flowers float at the end of long stalks. The fruits sink after flowering and ripen below the water surface. It is widespread, but commonest in W Scotland and W Ireland. It has suffered, along with other aquatics, from collection for the garden trade, and has been replaced in some areas by escaped garden plants. It is our largest wild flower.

J	F	M	A	M	J
J	A	S	O	N	D

Yellow Water-lily

Nuphar lutea

ID FACT FILE

Height: 1–2 m

Flowers: Yellow, 3–8 cm across, with 5–6 conspicuous sepals, much larger than the 20 or so petals; many large, yellow stamens

Leaves: Floating leaves circular, green, up to 40 cm across, rather leathery; underwater leaves thinner, crumpled

Fruits: Flask-like capsules, smelling somewhat of alcohol

Lookalikes: Fringed Water-lily (*Nymphoides peltata*), with smaller leaves and flowers, each with 5 fringed petals, is locally common in S and C England.

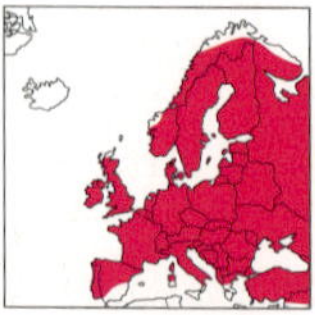

A hairless, aquatic perennial of still and slow-moving waters, arising from a massive corky rhizome and sometimes forming large patches. The leaves are both submerged and floating, at the end of long, spongy stalks; the flowers emerge several centimetres above the surface of the water. The fruits ripen above the water surface. This plant is a conspicuous, characteristic and attractive feature of many streams and rivers throughout Britain and Ireland, except for much of Scotland.

J	F	M	A	M	J
J	A	S	O	N	D

Marsh Marigold or Kingcup

Caltha palustris

ID FACT FILE

Height: 20–50 cm

Flowers: Golden yellow, shiny, 2–5 cm across, with 5 petal-like sepals and many yellow stamens

Leaves: Kidney- to heart-shaped, up to 10 cm across, dark green, the margins with neat, round teeth

Fruits: Group of 5–15 several-seeded, beaked fruits 10–18 mm long

Lookalikes: The buttercups (pp.35–39) have distinct sepals and petals, and 1-seeded fruits.

Hairless perennial with stout, hollow, branched stems, forming clumps and patches in marshes, damp fields, ditches and wet woods. Widespread but less common than formerly because of the drainage of wetlands and the destruction of old meadows by modern agriculture. The plant is poisonous and avoided by grazing animals. Plants in mountainous areas are small and the stems sometimes root; they flower later. Gardeners grow orange and double-flowered variants.

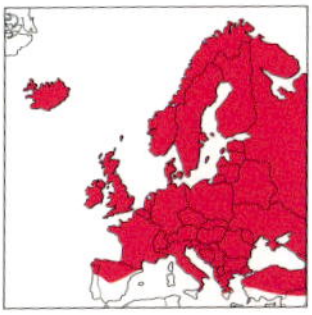

J	F	M	A	M	J
J	A	S	O	N	D

Until June in the mountains.

Wood Anemone

Anemone nemorosa

ID FACT FILE

HEIGHT: 8–25 cm

FLOWERS: Solitary, white, tinged pink or purple underneath, rarely lilac or blue, 2–4 cm across, with 5–7 (sometimes up to 12) petal-like sepals and many pale yellow stamens

LEAVES: Each with 3 much-divided and toothed lobes; stem leaves forming a protective ruff below the flower

FRUITS: 1-seeded, minutely hairy, in a round head

LOOKALIKES: Cultivated anemones, but these often have blue flowers.

Dainty, downy, erect perennial, with a creeping rhizome; locally common in open woodland, coppices and hedgerows, also meadows and mountain ledges. It is characteristic of surviving or former ancient woodland. It occurs through most of the British Isles, but is more local over much of Ireland and is absent from N Scotland. An attractive and early spring flower, it sometimes appears in great crowds, the flowers dancing in the breeze. The whole plant is poisonous.

J	F	M	A	M	J
J	A	S	O	N	D

Meadow Buttercup

Ranunculus acris

ID FACT FILE

Height: 30–100 cm

Flowers: Bright yellow, shiny, 15–25 mm across, with 5 petals, in loose, branched clusters; the sepals spreading

Leaves: Deeply divided into 3, 5 or 7 lobes, each deeply divided

Fruits: 1-seeded, with hooked beak, in a round head

Lookalikes: Other buttercups (pp.36–39). Bulbous Buttercup (p.36) has flowers with down-curved sepals; Creeping Buttercup (*Ranunculus repens*), with vigorous, rooting runners, grows in shadier places.

Erect, rather hairy perennial, a common plant of damp grassland, road-verges, woodland rides, marshes and mountain ledges. The commonest buttercup, sometimes colouring fields yellow, although less so than formerly owing to the destruction of old grassland by modern agriculture. The whole plant is poisonous, with acrid sap that can blister the skin. The burnished appearance of buttercup flowers is derived from light reflecting from starch grains within the structure of the petals.

J	F	M	A	M	J
J	A	S	O	N	D

Bulbous Buttercup

Ranunculus bulbosus

ID FACT FILE

Height: 10–50 cm

Flowers: Bright yellow, shiny, 2–3 cm across, 5 petals, solitary or in branched clusters; the sepals down-turned

Leaves: Deeply divided into 3 lobes, the middle one usually stalked, each divided, toothed

Fruits: 1-seeded, with curved beak, in a round head

Lookalikes: Creeping Buttercup (*Ranunculus repens*), with vigorous, rooting runners and spreading sepals, grows in damp places and is a weed. Meadow Buttercup (p.35) is taller, with dissected leaves and spreading sepals.

Erect, hairy perennial, with a conspicuously swollen stem-base or corm, found on well-drained soils rich in lime, especially in dry grassland and on sand-dunes. In N Scotland and Ireland it is more local and occurs only on the coasts. The earliest of the three common grassland buttercups to flower, this species has a short flowering season and the green shoots die down from midsummer until autumn. The whole plant is poisonous, with acrid sap that can blister the skin.

J	F	M	A	M	J
J	A	S	O	N	D

Lesser Celandine

Ranunculus ficaria

ID FACT FILE

Height: 5–30 cm

Flowers: Bright yellow, shiny, 15–30 mm across, with 8–12 rather narrow petals, solitary, opening only in bright sun; and 3 sepals

Leaves: Heart-shaped, rounded or blunt, deeply notched at base, shallowly toothed, often mottled with purplish or pale blotches

Fruits: Tiny, 1-seeded, without a beak, in a round head; often not developing

Lookalikes: The closely related buttercups and crowfoots (pp.35–40) have 5 sepals and divided leaves; they mostly flower later.

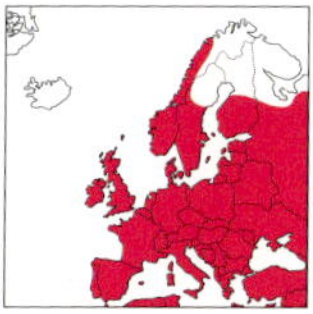

Low-growing, hairless perennial, forming extensive patches in damp places in woods, hedgerows, churchyards, gardens, banks of rivers and streams and sometimes grassland. The roots develop swollen tubers, which serve as a means of reproduction and, later in the season, tuber-like bulbils often develop in the angle of the leaf-stalks and stems. One of the very first flowers to appear at winter's end and a welcome sign of coming spring. The plant dies down by the end of June.

J	F	M	A	M	J
J	A	S	O	N	D

Lesser Spearwort

Ranunculus flammula

ID FACT FILE

Height: 10–50 cm

Flowers: Pale yellow, shiny, 8–20 mm across, with 5 petals

Leaves: Spear-shaped or narrowly oval, with untoothed or shallowly toothed margins

Fruits: 1-seeded, with short beak, in a round head

Lookalikes: Other buttercups (pp.35–39). Greater Spearwort (*Ranunculus lingua*), local in distribution, is much taller and more robust, with flowers 3–5 cm across.

Erect, ascending, sprawling or creeping, hairless perennial, the lower stems often reddish and hollow, rooting in the lower part. A common plant of marshes, bogs, damp grassland and the margins of ponds and lakes. It is poisonous, with acrid sap that can blister the skin; formerly used medicinally in Scotland. A very variable plant: two special variants of Lesser Spearwort, one erect with very narrow leaves, the other prostrate with round leaves, occur only in Scotland and W Ireland.

J	F	M	A	M	J
J	A	S	O	N	D

Celery-leaved Buttercup

Ranunculus sceleratus

ID FACT FILE

Height: 15–50 cm

Flowers: Pale yellow, shiny, 5–10 mm across, with 5 petals, in loose branched clusters

Leaves: Basal leaves deeply 3-lobed, the lobes divided; stem leaves less divided; all pale green, shiny

Fruits: Tiny, 1-seeded, hairless, in a short, cylindrical head

Lookalikes: Several buttercups have small, pale yellow flowers, although Celery-leaved Buttercup is the commonest.

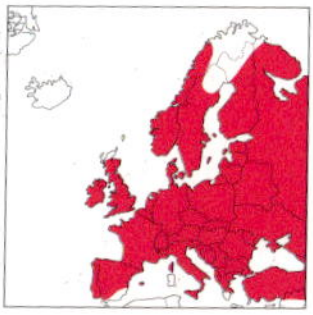

Erect, often much-branched, mostly hairless annual, with stout, hollow stems; a common plant of muddy, trampled and open places in marshes, damp grassland and the margins of ponds, lakes and rivers. It is poisonous, especially at flowering time, with acrid sap that has a bitter, burning taste and readily blisters the mouth and skin. This plant is the main cause of buttercup poisoning amongst farm animals; it is, however, safe to feed them hay containing dried buttercups.

J	F	M	A	M	J
J	A	S	O	N	D

Pond Water-crowfoot

Ranunculus peltatus

ID FACT FILE

Height: 10–50 cm

Flowers: Solitary, on stalks 50 mm or more long, white, shiny, 15–30 mm across, with 5 petals, each yellow-spotted at the base

Leaves: Floating leaves kidney-shaped or almost round, 5-lobed (sometimes 3- or 7-lobed), glossy; submerged leaves divided into thread-like segments

Fruits: 1-seeded, with small beak, hairy, in a round head

Lookalikes: Water-crowfoots differ from buttercups by their white, not yellow flowers.

Trailing, aquatic perennial that can form large populations in still, unpolluted waters of slow streams, lakes and ponds. The flowers, emerging on long, erect stalks above the surface of the water, can be an impressive sight on a sunny day. This is one of a group of ten or so water-crowfoots that occur in Britain and Ireland: some in still or slowly flowing water, with both floating and submerged leaves; some in fast-flowing water, with submerged leaves only; others on mud, without submerged leaves.

J	F	M	A	M	J
J	A	S	O	N	D

Traveller's Joy or Old Man's Beard

Clematis vitalba

ID FACT FILE

Height: 1–10 m

Flowers: Solitary, on stalks 5 cm or more long, without petals, but with 4 greenish-cream sepals and many cream stamens

Leaves: In opposite pairs, compound, each with usually 5 leaflets; the leaf-stalks twine around twigs and other supports

Fruits: 1-seeded, with a plume derived from stigma, in a round head

Lookalikes: Related garden species, with larger, coloured flowers, sometimes escape and become established in the wild.

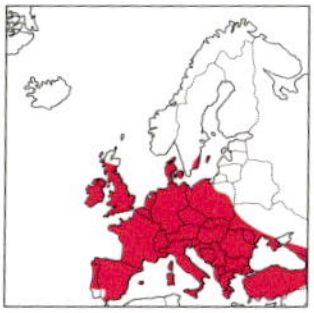

Woody climbing shrub, scrambling untidily over hedges, scrub and banks, and high into the branches of trees. The old stems often form great looping lianes in woods, the bark peeling off in strings. The fluffy seed-heads are a conspicuous, cheering feature of the autumn and winter landscape. This plant is characteristic of soils on chalk and limestone in S Britain, extending to N Wales and much of the Midlands; it is introduced further north and here and there in Ireland.

J	F	M	A	M	J
J	A	S	O	N	D

Common, or Corn, Poppy

Papaver rhoeas

ID FACT FILE

Height: 20–80 cm

Flowers: Solitary, on long stalks, rich scarlet, flimsy, 5–10 cm across; many bluish-black stamens; the 2 sepals fall off

Leaves: Compound, divided into many toothed lobes

Fruits: Smooth, nearly spherical capsules 1–2 cm long, which release seed from a ring of pores – like a pepper pot

Lookalikes: Long-headed Poppy (*Papaver dubium*) has club-shaped capsules up to 25 mm long and paler-scarlet flowers. Two other, rarer, poppies have bristly fruits.

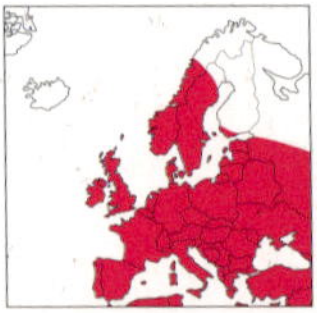

A hairy annual, with erect or ascending, bristly stems. The plant sometimes appears in great crowds, colouring cornfields and other arable land, new road-verges, allotments and waste ground red, especially on lime-rich soils in S and E England. Seed can persist in the soil for decades, germinating on exposure to light. Poppies (and other weeds) covered the disturbed chalk soil of the Somme and other battlefields after 1916, becoming a symbol of the carnage. When cut, the stems and leaves exude a white juice.

J	F	M	A	M	J
J	A	S	O	N	D

Horned Poppy

Glaucium flavum

ID FACT FILE

Height: 30–100 cm

Flowers: Solitary, yellow, flimsy, 5–9 cm across, with 4 petals and many yellow stamens; the 2 sepals fall off

Leaves: Silvery-grey, bristly, deeply lobed with toothed margins; upper leaves clasping stems

Fruits: Unmistakable, smooth, slender, curved, cylindrical capsules up to 30 cm long

Lookalikes: Welsh Poppy (*Meconopsis cambrica*) of shady places in W Britain and Ireland, a garden escape in N Britain, has green leaves and capsules 2–4 cm long.

A distinctive and conspicuous, silvery-grey, branched biennial or perennial of shingle beaches and coastal sands. The stems and leaves exude a yellow sap when cut. This handsome plant, which is erratic in appearance but locally abundant, is a distinctive feature of less disturbed coastal beaches in the summer, as far north as the Firths of Clyde and Forth in C Scotland; it is more local in Ireland. It occurs inland as a weed in the Mediterranean region, but only rarely so in Britain.

J	F	M	A	M	J
J	A	S	O	N	D

Greater Celandine

Chelidonium majus

ID FACT FILE

Height: 20–80 cm

Flowers: Yellow, flimsy, 20–25 mm across, with 4 petals and 2 sepals; 2–8 in loose, domed clusters; many yellow stamens

Leaves: Compound, with 5–9 bluntly toothed leaflets, slightly greyish-green beneath

Fruits: Smooth, cylindrical capsules 3–5 cm long

Lookalikes: Welsh Poppy (*Meconopsis cambrica*) – native in rocky and shady places in W Britain and elsewhere an escape from gardens – has solitary flowers up to 4 cm across.

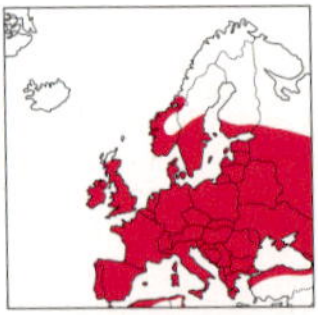

A tufted perennial of walls, hedge-banks and shady waste ground. Although apparently native on some rocky woodland banks, it is rarely found far away from houses or ruins; it is local and certainly introduced in Scotland and Ireland. When cut, the stems and leaves exude an acrid, orange juice, which has been used to treat warts and also, more surprisingly perhaps, sore eyes. Lesser Celandine (p.37) is an unrelated and quite different plant of the buttercup family.

J	F	M	A	M	J
J	A	S	O	N	D

All through mild winters.

Common Fumitory

Fumaria officinalis

ID FACT FILE

Height: 1–100 cm

Flowers: Purplish-pink, about 10 mm long, 10–50 in rather dense spikes 2–8 cm long

Leaves: Compound, deeply divided, lobed and feathery, somewhat greyish

Fruits: 1-seeded, almost spherical nutlets, 2–2.5 mm across

Lookalikes: Other fumitories. The stems do not exude the white or yellow juice of the poppies.

Branched, hairless, sprawling or weakly climbing annual of cultivated land, new road-verges and waste ground. Fumitories comprise a dozen or so similar species that are all closely associated with cultivated and disturbed ground. Several are rare and two species are restricted to Britain and Ireland, being found nowhere else in the world. They are related to the poppies (pp.42–43) but have clustered, bilaterally symmetrical rather than few or solitary, radially symmetrical flowers.

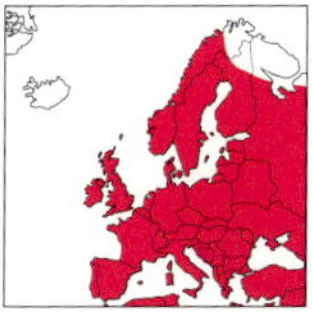

J	F	M	A	M	J
J	A	S	O	N	D

Hedge Mustard

Sisymbrium officinale

ID FACT FILE

Height: 20–100 cm

Flowers: Petals 2–4 mm, pale yellow; flowers in narrow spikes, lengthening considerably as the fruits develop

Leaves: Deeply cut into spear-shaped lobes, the terminal one larger and triangular

Fruits: Short, tapered pods up to 20 mm long, closely pressed to the stem

Lookalikes: Other members of the family with yellow flowers; the pale yellow colour is distinctive.

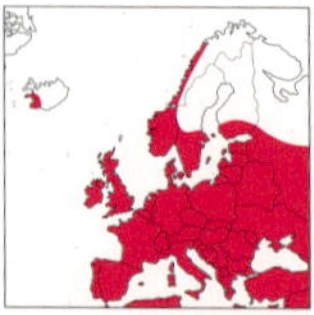

Roughly downy annual, or biennial, with stiff, widely spreading branches. A common plant of waste places and hedge-banks, also in gardens and on cultivated land, it is widespread throughout most of Britain and Ireland, although scarce in N Scotland. This familiar but not terribly attractive plant is easily recognised by the tiny clusters of pale yellow flowers atop the long, narrow fruiting spikes. Like most members of the cabbage and cress family, the plant has an acrid, mustard taste.

J	F	M	A	M	J
J	A	S	O	N	D

All through mild winters.

Shepherd's Purse

Capsella bursa-pastoris

ID FACT FILE

Height: 5–60 cm

Flowers: 2–3 mm across, in long, slender spikes; petals white, longer than the green or pink calyx

Leaves: Oblong or spear-shaped, deeply cut into pointed lobes, the end one larger, triangular; upper leaves few, arrow-shaped, clasping the stem

Fruits: Small, flattened, triangular or heart-shaped pods, each like a little purse

Lookalikes: Field Penny-cress (p.48) has more showy flowers and much larger, circular fruits.

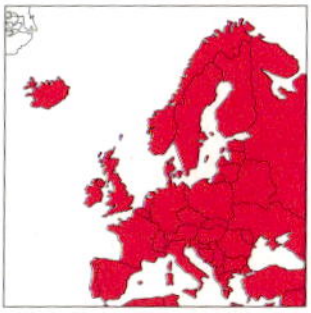

An erect, downy, branched annual, with a neat rosette of basal leaves. Abundant on cultivated and waste ground and perhaps the commonest and most familiar of all weeds. It is one of the first flowers of late winter and early spring, along with Chickweed (p.25), Red Dead-nettle (p.154) and Groundsel (p.215). In winter the stems and pods are attacked by white fungus, which covers and distorts them. A very variable species, especially in the size of the flowers and shape of the pods and leaves.

J	F	M	A	M	J
J	A	S	O	N	D

Field Penny-cress

Thlaspi arvense

ID FACT FILE

Height: 10–50 cm

Flowers: Petals 2–3 mm, white; flowers in flat clusters, elongating as the fruits develop

Leaves: Oblong or spear-shaped, slightly glossy, pale green; stem leaves clasping, arrow-shaped at base

Fruits: Flattened, almost circular, broadly winged and deeply notched pods up to 15 mm long

Lookalikes: Shepherd's Purse (p.47) has smaller flowers and much smaller triangular or heart-shaped fruits.

Hairless, little-branched annual, sometimes abundant on cultivated ground and waysides. The whole plant, but notably the distinctive fruits, has a foetid, garlic smell when crushed. It is a widespread, if rather local, plant in Britain, found mostly south of a Severn-Wash line; scarce in Ireland. There are three species of penny-cress native to Britain; most of the European species are perennials of mountain rocks, especially on soils rich in metals such as lead and zinc.

J	F	M	A	M	J
J	A	S	O	N	D

Garlic Mustard or Jack-by-the-Hedge

Alliaria petiolata

ID FACT FILE

Height: 30–120 cm

Flowers: Petals 2–3 mm, white; flowers in domed clusters, elongating as the fruits develop

Leaves: Long-stalked, oval or triangular, with heart-shaped base, deeply toothed

Fruits: Slightly 4-angled, cylindrical pods 2–7 cm long, on short, stiff, spreading stalks

Lookalikes: The heart-shaped leaves and garlic smell distinguish this plant from other members of the family with white flowers.

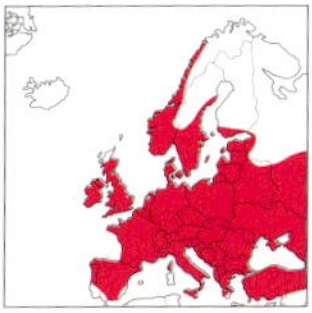

An almost hairless, robust biennial, or short-lived perennial, smelling strongly of garlic when bruised. Common in hedgerows, woodland margins, shady banks, churchyards and gardens. Its rather stiff, upright habit and white flowers make the plant a feature of waysides in May. This is one of the food plants of Orange Tip and Green-veined White butterflies. Garlic Mustard and a few species of penny-cress are remarkable for their garlic smell, which is rare outside the onion family.

J	F	M	A	M	J
J	A	S	O	N	D

Wallflower

Erysimum cheiri

ID FACT FILE

Height: 20–60 cm

Flowers: 20–25 mm across, richly scented, the petals yellow or sometimes orange or streaked with red

Leaves: Narrow, spear-shaped, almost stalkless, covered with minute, branched, flattened hairs

Fruits: Slightly flattened, cylindrical pods, 2–8 cm long, on short, stiff, semi-erect stalk

Lookalikes: Hoary Stock (*Matthiola incana*), rare on sea-cliffs, also a garden escape, has greyish leaves and purplish flowers.

A bushy biennial or perennial, sometimes rather shrubby, that brightens walls, old ruins, cliffs, railway cuttings and quarries. It is not native, but has a garden origin and probably arose as a cross between closely related Greek species. It is now well established in rocky habitats all over W Europe. Plants in the wild mostly have yellow flowers, but in the garden there is a greater range of colour. Gardeners usually grow the plants as biennials, discarding them after flowering.

J	F	M	A	M	J
J	A	S	O	N	D

Charlock or Wild Mustard

Sinapis arvensis

ID FACT FILE

Height: 20–60 cm

Flowers: 14–18 mm across, golden-yellow, in tall, loose clusters

Leaves: Lyre-shaped, irregularly lobed and raggedly toothed; upper leaves narrow, toothed

Fruits: Cylindrical pods, up to 5 cm long, constricted between the seeds, with a conical beak; seeds reddish-brown

Lookalikes: White Mustard (*Sinapis alba*), cultivated as a crop and persisting as a weed, has more divided leaves and the pods have flattened beaks; it is less common.

Roughly and stiffly hairy, usually branched, annual of cultivated and waste ground, widespread, especially on lighter soils. The seeds can persist for decades in the soil and plants may appear in huge numbers on disturbed ground. Modern herbicides now control this weed amongst crops. It was formerly cooked and eaten as a late winter vegetable, as it still is (together with several other members of the cabbage and cress family) in Greece and elsewhere.

J	F	M	A	M	J
J	A	S	O	N	D

Scurvy-grass

Cochlearia officinalis

ID FACT FILE

Height: 10–50 cm

Flowers: 6–10 mm across, white or sometimes pale lilac, scented, in loose domed clusters

Leaves: Kidney-shaped, or almost round, fleshy, dark green

Fruits: Small, globular pods, becoming corky when ripe

Lookalikes: Early Scurvy-grass (*Cochlearia danica)* is smaller and annual, with often lilac flowers and egg-shaped pods, occurring on open ground by the sea, and inland by railways and abundantly along roads.

Rather stout, hairless biennial with erect or ascending stems, of coastal cliffs, rocks and saltmarshes, and walls, road-verges and banks by the sea. It is locally common, making extensive splashes of white in spring, although absent from much of the south coast. The leaves, rich in vitamin C, were formerly eaten as a winter green and to stave off scurvy. A very variable species; distinctive plants are found on mountains in Wales, N Britain and Ireland.

Lady's Smock or Cuckooflower

Cardamine pratensis

J	F	M	A	M	J
J	A	S	O	N	D

ID FACT FILE

Height: 20–40 cm

Flowers: 1–2 cm across, lilac or almost white, in loose clusters

Leaves: Neatly compound, the leaflets slightly toothed, the terminal one larger; stem leaves smaller, with narrower lobes

Fruits: Cylindrical pods, 2–4 cm long, exploding to disperse the seeds

Lookalikes: Sea Rocket (*Cakile maritima*), also with lilac or whitish flowers, is an annual plant of seashores that has fleshy leaves and short, very stout fruits.

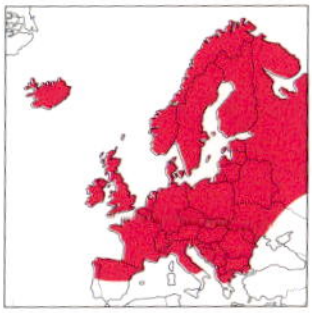

A dainty, erect perennial of marshy ground, damp grassland and woodland rides, also on mountain ledges and even damp lawns. It has long been welcomed as a symbol both pure and sensual of spring, flowering as it does, in John Gerard's evocative description in his 1597 *Herball*: 'for the most part in April and May, when the Cuckoo begins to sing her pleasant note'. A particularly attractive, double-flowered variant, prized by gardeners, can sometimes be found in the wild.

J	F	M	A	M	J
J	A	S	O	N	D

Hairy Bitter-cress

Cardamine hirsuta

ID FACT FILE

Height: 5–25 cm

Flowers: 2–3 mm across, white, in branched clusters; 4 stamens

Leaves: Mostly in a basal rosette, compound, with 1–5 pairs of leaflets; stem leaves smaller

Fruits: Erect, cylindrical pods, 18–25 mm long, exploding violently to disperse the seeds

Lookalikes: Thale Cress (*Arabidopsis thaliana*), another hairy, white-flowered weed of cultivated ground and walls, is more slender, with undivided, toothed leaves and very narrow pods.

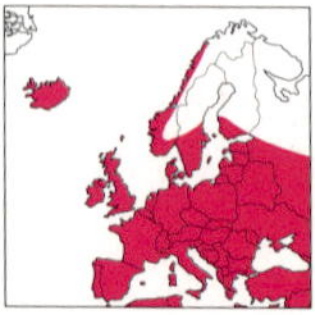

Erect, not particularly hairy, usually small, annual of cultivated and waste ground, paths and walls, also on rocks and sand-dunes away from human activity. The explosive splitting of the pods ensures good seed dispersal, which makes this plant an irritating weed of the garden, nursery and glasshouse. There are three other species of bitter-cress, together with the closely related Lady's Smock (p.53), in Britain, and several more in Europe.

J	F	M	A	M	J
J	A	S	O	N	D

Water Cress

Nasturtium officinale

ID FACT FILE

Height: 10–50 cm

Flowers: 4–5 mm across, white, in loose clusters; 6 stamens

Leaves: Compound, with 1–4 pairs of blunt, only slightly toothed leaflets

Fruits: Straight or slightly curved, cylindrical pods, 12–18 mm; seeds many, in 2 rows

Lookalikes: The wet habitat distinguishes this from other white-flowered members of the cabbage and cress family; Lady's Smock (p.53) sometimes occurs in wet marshes.

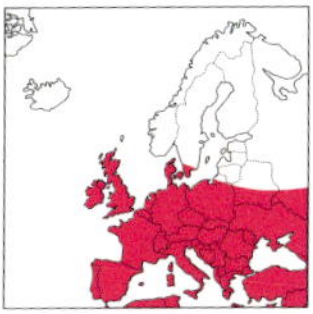

Creeping or floating, branched, hairless, aquatic perennial, rooting readily in streams, ditches with running water, and on open mud. In England this plant has been cultivated since the 19th century in clear, unpolluted spring water. The pungent flavour, characteristic of members of the cabbage and cress family, derives from mustard oils. Like Scurvy-grass (p.52), Water Cress was a preventative remedy for scurvy, as plants remain green in winter when salads are scarce.

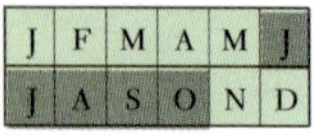

Weld or Dyer's Greenweed

Reseda luteola

ID FACT FILE

Height: 50–100 cm

Flowers: Pale yellow, many, in 10–30 cm spike; 4 petals 2–4 mm long, and 20–30 stamens

Leaves: Strap-shaped, glossy, with wavy margins

Fruits: Nearly spherical capsules with black, shiny seeds

Lookalikes: Wild Mignonette (p.57) has deeply divided leaves, 6 petals and 12–20 stamens.

An erect, little-branched biennial of dry banks, fallow fields, roadsides, railway sidings and waste places, especially on lime-rich soils; widespread, although commoner in the east and rare over much of Scotland. It is sometimes abundant on new road verges. The plant has long been used as the source of bright green and yellow dyes and is sometimes grown in gardens. The fruits, and those of Wild Mignonette (p.57), are unusual because they are not fully closed, even before they are ripe.

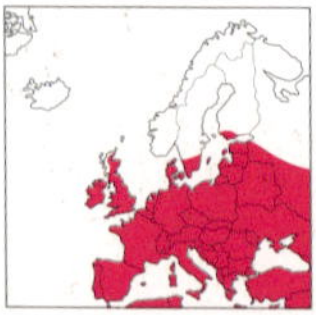

J	F	M	A	M	J
J	A	S	O	N	D

Wild Mignonette

Reseda lutea

ID FACT FILE

Height: 30–80 cm

Flowers: Pale yellow in 5–20 cm spikes; 6 petals, 3–4 mm long, and 12–20 stamens

Leaves: Deeply divided and lobed, pale green

Fruits: Cylindrical capsules with black, shiny seeds

Lookalikes: Weld (p.56) has strap-shaped leaves, 4 petals and 20–30 stamens.

A sprawling, often rather untidy, branched annual, biennial or perennial of disturbed ground, roadsides and waste places, usually on lime-rich soil, especially chalk. It is less frequent in the west and is rare in Scotland; in Ireland it occurs mainly near the east coast. The English name derives from its similarity to the scented Mignonette (*Reseda odorata*) of old-fashioned cottage gardens. The fruits, and those of Weld (p.56), are unusual because they are not fully closed, even before they are ripe.

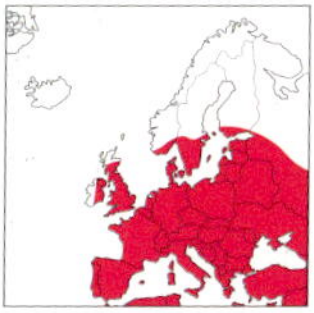

J	F	M	A	M	J
J	A	S	O	N	D

Round-leaved Sundew

Drosera rotundifolia

ID FACT FILE

Height: 3–8 cm

Flowers: 5 mm across, white, with 6 petals, in small clusters atop a slender stem

Leaves: All in a basal rosette, stalked, reddish, almost round, shorter than the flowering stem; each covered with long, sticky-tipped hairs that trap and bend over to digest small insects

Fruits: Small, smooth capsules

Lookalikes: Oblong-leaved Sundew (*Drosera intermedia*) has narrowly oval leaves; Great Sundew (*Drosera anglica*) is larger, with narrowly oval leaves.

Distinctive, small, tufted perennial with a remarkable ability to entrap, digest and absorb small insects to supplement its mineral requirements. A plant of acid bogs, especially in the north and west, it grows on bare peat or on sopping carpets of bog-moss, sometimes in huge crowds. The trapping of insects, as with Common Butterwort (p.183), is a nutritional adaptation to the low mineral levels in bogs. This plant is rare in the lowlands, where it is threatened by extraction of peat for horticulture.

J	F	M	A	M	J
J	A	S	O	N	D

Wall Pennywort or Navelwort

Umbilicus rupestris

ID FACT FILE

Height: 10–80 cm

Flowers: Up to 1 cm long, tubular, greenish-yellow or reddish, hanging, massed in long, slender spikes

Leaves: Mostly in a basal rosette, long-stalked, 3–8 cm across, round with a central depression, very fleshy, hairless; stem leaves spoon- or wedge-shaped

Fruits: Fused clusters of 5 enclosed in the enlarged, persistent flower

Lookalikes: Another fleshy plant, Orpine (*Sedum telephium*), has toothed, oval leaves and domed heads of pink or white flowers.

A fleshy, hairless, tufted perennial, rather woody at the base, with stout erect flowering stems, locally common on cliffs, rocks, walls, hedge-banks and even, further west, on the branches and crooks of trees. A conspicuous and unusual-looking plant, rather irresistible to the touch. It is found northwards to Mull and is mostly western in distribution, being frost-sensitive, although it occurs for example in the Weald of S England. It is absent from much of the Irish midlands.

J	F	M	A	M	J
J	A	S	O	N	D

Biting Stonecrop

Sedum acre

ID FACT FILE

Height: 10–80 cm

Flowers: Starry, bright yellow, with 5 petals, up to 10 mm across, in terminal clusters

Leaves: Very fleshy, narrowly egg-shaped; sharp, peppery taste

Fruits: Fused clusters of 5 enclosed in the enlarged, persistent flower

Lookalikes: Other stonecrops, most of them escaped from gardens.

A low-growing, fleshy perennial, with erect shoots and flowering-stems, forming extensive patches on sand-dunes, shingle beaches, walls, railway ballast and waysides. In midsummer this plant provides spectacular splashes of yellow on disused or neglected railway sidings, concrete tracks, former airfields and car-parks. The leaves often have a red tinge, caused by lack of nutrients in the shallow soils. An alternative, if obscure, English name is 'Welcome-home-husband-however-drunk-you-be'!

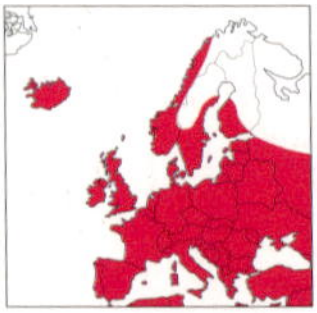

J	F	M	A	M	J
J	A	S	O	N	D

Meadow Saxifrage

Saxifraga granulata

ID FACT FILE

Height: 10–50 cm

Flowers: 15 mm across, white, with 5 petals and sticky-hairy sepals, in small clusters atop almost leafless stems

Leaves: Mostly in a basal rosette, stalked, almost round, with lobed margins and long hairs

Fruits: 2-lobed capsules, each lobe with a horn-like, persistent stigma

Lookalikes: Rue-leaved Saxifrage (*Saxifraga tridactylites*) is a smaller, annual plant, with 3- to 5-lobed leaves, of walls and dry grassland; other saxifrages grow on damp mountain rocks.

An elegant, rather sticky-hairy, erect perennial, of well-drained grassland on lime-rich soil. It used to be more common before modern farming destroyed old meadows, but can still be found here and there on dry roadside banks and especially in country churchyards. It occurs mainly in E and S England; it is scarce in Scotland and very rare indeed in Ireland. Small tuber-like bulbils at the base of the leaves allow the plant to reproduce vegetatively as well as by seed.

J	F	M	A	M	J
J	A	S	O	N	D

Grass-of-Parnassus

Parnassia palustris

ID FACT FILE

Height: 10–50 cm

Flowers: Solitary, white, veined with green, 15–30 mm across, scented, with 5 petals; 5 stamens, also 5 fringed structures that attract insects

Leaves: Mostly in basal rosette, long-stalked, heart-shaped; 1 single, clasping stem leaf

Fruits: Egg-shaped capsules 12–20 mm long, splitting into 4 segments

Lookalikes: Unlikely to be confused with any other plant.

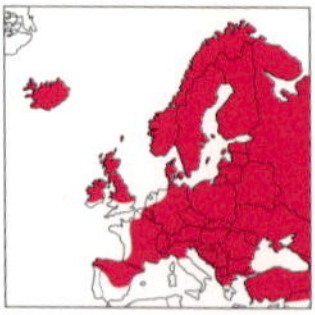

One of our most beautiful wild flowers: an erect, hairless perennial with several flowering stems, of marshes, wet heaths, and damp places in sand-dunes. It is local in distribution, absent from much of S England, Wales and SW Ireland; it has become extinct in the English Midlands as a result of the drainage and destruction of wetlands. This is the only European species of a N-hemisphere group of some 15 species. Plants from sand-dunes are shorter and have slightly larger flowers.

J	F	M	A	M	J
J	A	S	O	N	D

Meadowsweet

Filipendula ulmaria

ID FACT FILE

Height: 50–120 cm, sometimes up to 200 cm

Flowers: Creamy-white, 4–8 mm across, scented, in wide, dense, branched, frothy clusters

Leaves: Compound, with up to 5 pairs of large leaflets, smaller leaflets between, and a 3- to 5-lobed terminal leaflet, all white-hairy beneath

Fruits: Few-seeded, in clusters of 6–10

Lookalikes: Dropwort (*Filipendula vulgaris*), of dry grassland on limestone, has leaves with 8–20 pairs of leaflets, and fewer flowers 8–18 mm across.

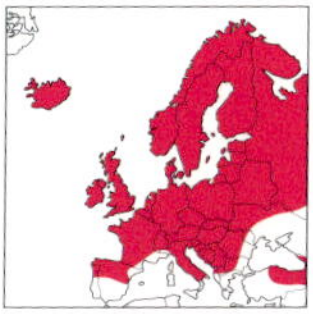

Erect, leafy, hairy perennial, with a creeping rhizome, a widespread and often abundant plant of damp grassland, marshes, streamsides and wet, open woods. In summer, with its frothy clusters of flowers, it is one of Britain's most conspicuous wild flowers, especially in the west. In earlier times it was popularly strewn on the floors of buildings to sweeten the air, although the flowers have a rather sickly scent; it has also been used medicinally in the treatment of arthritis and rheumatism.

J	F	M	A	M	J
J	A	S	O	N	D

Dog Rose

Rosa canina

ID FACT FILE

Height: 1–3 m

Flowers: Varying shades of pink, 2–6 cm across, with 5 petals and many stamens

Leaves: Compound with 3–5 oval, toothed, green leaflets

Fruits: Fleshy, flask-shaped or almost globular, scarlet or pale orange, topped by dry remains of flower

Lookalikes: Field Rose (*Rosa arvensis*) is up to 1 m tall and has white flowers; Burnet Rose (*Rosa pimpinellifolia*), forming clumps of densely prickly stems on sand-dunes and heaths, has smaller white flowers.

An arched shrub, the stems armed with ferocious, curved prickles. One of the best-loved of all wild flowers, brightening hedges with great splashes of pink in June. There are some dozen or so closely related species of wild rose in Britain and Ireland, all loosely termed dog roses, together with hybrids; several garden roses also escape and cross with native species. Dog Rose was formerly used as a stock for grafting garden roses, but other species are now used. The fruits are rich in vitamin C.

J	F	M	A	M	J
J	A	S	O	N	D

Bramble or Blackberry

Rubus fruticosus

ID FACT FILE

Height: 1–4 m, but mostly trailing

Flowers: White, pink or purplish-pink, 2–3 cm across, with 5 petals and many stamens

Leaves: With 3 oval, coarsely toothed, green leaflets, paler beneath

Fruits: Fleshy, globular heads, 1–2 cm across, of black, 1-seeded drupes

Lookalikes: Wild Raspberry (*Rubus idaeus*) has erect stems, leaflets in pairs and red, softer fruits.

An arched, prickly shrub, forming a tangle of stems near the ground and climbing into bushes and hedges. Common and widespread, it can be a serious weed of woods and waste ground, although it provides cover and food for many animals. The fruits are an ever-popular source of free food and the roots yield an orange dye; the leaves have been used to treat wounds and appear in herbal teas. Botanists divide Blackberry up into hundreds of similar 'micro-species', many of them very local in distribution.

J	F	M	A	M	J
J	A	S	O	N	D

Agrimony

Agrimonia eupatoria

ID FACT FILE

Height: 30–150 cm

Flowers: 6–8 mm across, with 5 yellow petals and 10–20 stamens, massed in a long spike

Leaves: Basal leaves in a rosette; leaves compound, with 6–8 pairs of large and 2–3 pairs of smaller leaflets, all greyish-hairy beneath

Fruits: In shape of inverted cone (like an old-fashioned top), grooved, half enclosed by the cup-like calyx, covered with hooked bristles

Lookalikes: The tall spikes of yellow flowers and bristly fruits are distinctive.

Erect, softly hairy perennial of road verges, hedgerows, scrub, woodland margins and tall grassland; conspicuous in late summer. It is widespread, but is scarce over much of Scotland, especially the north. The hooked spines of the persistent calyx that surrounds the ripe fruit readily attach themselves to fur or clothing and fruits are thus dispersed far from the parent plant. The plant yields a yellow dye and has long been used medicinally as an antiseptic and general tonic.

J	F	M	A	M	J
J	A	S	O	N	D

Salad Burnet

Sanguisorba minor

ID FACT FILE

Height: 20–90 cm

Flowers: Green, reddish or purplish in small globular heads up to 1 cm across; the petals are replaced by a 4-lobed calyx

Leaves: Basal leaves in a rosette; leaves greyish-green, compound, with 3–12 pairs of oval, sharply toothed leaflets

Fruits: 1-seeded, enclosed in persistent, 4-angled, wrinkled calyx, in small round clusters

Lookalikes: Great Burnet (*Sanguisorba officinalis*), a larger plant that has 1–3 cm oblong heads of red flowers, occurs in damp meadows.

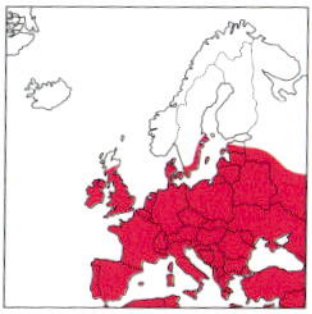

Erect, hairless to somewhat downy perennial of dry grassland, rocky places and cliffs on limestone. It is especially characteristic of the chalk grassland of S England, but occurs northwards to C Scotland. The flowers are pollinated by wind rather than insects, which is unusual in the rose family. Robust plants, with larger, more wrinkled fruits, occur on road-verges and recently sown grassland. A former fodder crop, these are now distributed with commercial wild flower seed.

J	F	M	A	M	J
J	A	S	O	N	D

Wood Avens

Geum urbanum

ID FACT FILE

Height: 20–60 cm

Flowers: Shallowly cup-shaped, yellow, 10–15 mm across, the calyx green; many stamens

Leaves: Basal leaves in a rosette; leaves compound, with 1–5 pairs of unequal leaflets

Fruits: Round cluster of hairy, 1-seeded fruits, each with a persistent, hooked stigma

Lookalikes: Water Avens (p.69) has larger, nodding, bell-shaped, pink flowers and grows in damper places.

An erect, branched, leafy perennial of open woodland, woodland margins and rides, hedgerows and shady gardens; widespread, but local in N Scotland. The flowers are pollinated by flies. The long hooks on the fruits attach themselves to fur or clothing and the fruits are thus dispersed far from the parent plant. This species often crosses with Water Avens (p.69) in W and N Britain, with hybrids and backcrosses displaying a mixture of the features of both parents.

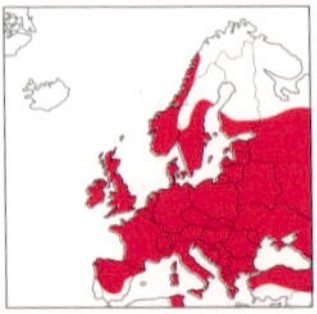

J	F	M	A	M	J
J	A	S	O	N	D

Water Avens

Geum rivale

ID FACT FILE

Height: 20–40 cm

Flowers: Pink, nodding, 10–15 mm long, the calyx brownish-purple; many stamens

Leaves: Basal leaves in a rosette; leaves compound, with 3–6 pairs of unequal leaflets

Fruits: Round cluster of hairy, 1-seeded fruits, each with a persistent, hooked stigma

Lookalikes: Wood Avens (p.68) has smaller, cup-shaped, yellow flowers and grows in drier places.

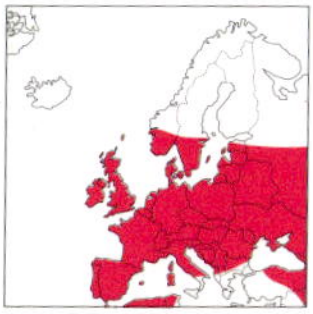

An erect, branched, leafy perennial of woods, hedgerows and damp, shady places. It is widespread, but commoner in N and W Britain; it is rather scattered in Ireland. The flowers are pollinated by bumblebees. The long hooks on the fruits attach themselves to fur or clothing and fruits are thus dispersed far from the parent plant. This species often crosses with Wood Avens (p.68) in W and N Britain; hybrids and backcrosses show a mixture of features of both parents.

J	F	M	A	M	J
J	A	S	O	N	D

Silverweed

Potentilla anserina

ID FACT FILE

Height: 10–30 cm

Flowers: Golden yellow, 15–20 mm across, with 5 petals and many stamens, solitary on long stems

Leaves: Leaves all in a basal rosette, compound, with 7–25 coarsely toothed, oblong or oval leaflets, silvery-hairy beneath

Fruits: Head of small, round achenes

Lookalikes: Creeping Cinquefoil (*Potentilla reptans*) is a more slender, far-creeping plant, with green leaves and leaflets grouped in fives.

Silvery-hairy, prostrate perennial with far-creeping, red, rooting stems, forming extensive patches. Abundant in damp, grassy places, waste ground and seashores near the point reached by the highest tides. The fleshy roots were formerly extensively eaten, and were a staple during times of famine, especially in N and W Britain and in Ireland; it may even have been truly cultivated in highland regions. The plant has been used for its healing properties.

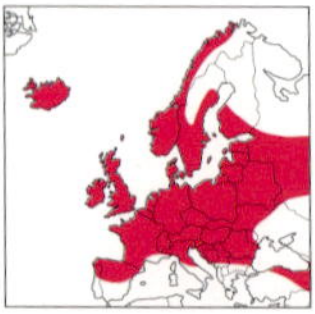

J	F	M	A	M	J
J	A	S	O	N	D

Tormentil

Potentilla erecta

ID FACT FILE

HEIGHT: 10–40 cm

FLOWERS: Yellow, 8–18 mm across, with 4 (rarely 5) petals and sepals and many stamens; grouped in loose, leafy clusters

LEAVES: Leaves mostly in a basal rosette, which often withers by flowering time, with 3–5 spear-shaped, sharply toothed leaflets

FRUITS: Round head of minute, hairless 1-seeded fruits

LOOKALIKES: Creeping Cinquefoil (*Potentilla reptans*) has creeping runners, leaves with 5–7 leaflets, and 4-petalled flowers 15–35 mm across.

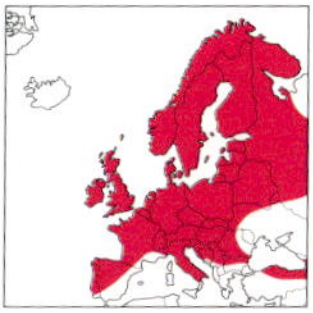

A dainty perennial with slender, sprawling, ascending or weakly erect stems, common in bogs, damp grassland, birch woods, moors and heaths, especially in hilly districts and in the mountains. Its presence always indicates that the soil is acid, i.e. very low in lime. The rather woody roots yield a red dye and were formerly used in tanning. The plant sometimes forms intermediate hybrids with Creeping Cinquefoil (see LOOKALIKES).

J	F	M	A	M	J
J	A	S	O	N	D

Barren Strawberry

Potentilla sterilis

ID FACT FILE

Height: 5–15 cm

Flowers: White, 10–15 mm across, with 5 petals and sepals and a conspicuous ring of orange nectaries; many stamens

Leaves: Leaves mostly in basal rosettes, with 3 oval, coarsely toothed, greyish-green leaflets

Fruits: Round head of minute 1-seeded fruits

Lookalikes: Wild Strawberry (p.73) has bright green leaves, long runners and fleshy, scarlet fruits; it flowers in early summer.

Tufted, low-growing, hairy perennial of dry grassland, hedge-banks, churchyards and open woods. It is one of the very first flowers of late winter and early spring. It is widespread and common, although absent from N Scotland, but frequently overlooked and often confused with the true Wild Strawberry (p.73). John Gerard in his 1597 *Herball* described the fruits rather well, if unkindly, as 'a barren or chaffie head, in shape like a Strawberrie, but of no worth or value'!

J	F	M	A	M	J
J	A	S	O	N	D

Wild Strawberry

Fragaria vesca

ID FACT FILE

Height: 5–30 cm

Flowers: White, 10–18 mm across, with 5 petals and sepals and many stamens

Leaves: Leaves mostly in basal rosettes, with 3 oval, coarsely toothed, green leaflets

Fruits: Fleshy, globular, scarlet heads 10–15 mm across, studded with minute 1-seeded fruits

Lookalikes: Barren Strawberry (p.72) has greyish-green leaves, shorter runners, and minute, dry fruits; it flowers in early spring.

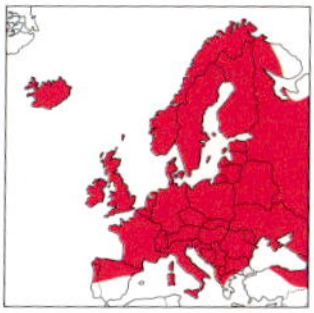

Softly hairy perennial with long, slender, reddish runners; a common plant of open woods, scrub, sunny banks and waste ground. It is particularly abundant where vegetation is regenerating after beech woodland over chalk has been felled. No longer gathered commercially, the sweet fruits are still a popular free product of the countryside. The much larger garden strawberries (*Fragaria ananassa*) mostly derive from a cross between two cultivated New World species.

J	F	M	A	M	J
J	A	S	O	N	D

All through mild winters.

Gorse or Furze

Ulex europaeus

ID FACT FILE

Height: 50–300 cm

Flowers: Richly vanilla-scented, golden yellow, 15–20 mm long, in short, dense clusters

Leaves: On young plants, each with 3 spear-shaped or narrowly oval leaflets; on mature plants reduced to spines

Fruits: Flattened pods 15–20 mm, black, hairy

Lookalikes: Broom (p.75) has no spines and has longer, less hairy pods. Dwarf Gorse (*Ulex gallii*) is smaller and flowers in late summer.

Hairy, dense, spiny shrub, forming impenetrable thickets on heaths, cliffs and rough grassland and on derelict railway lines or industrial land. In spring the flowers can scent the air, and on a hot day in summer the pods can be heard to open explosively with a distinct crackling pop. The plant was formerly cut as an important source of fuel, ideal for kindling, and for animal fodder. The proverb 'When gorse's out of bloom, kissing's out of season' derives from the long flowering season with always a few flowers present through the winter.

J	F	M	A	M	J
J	A	S	O	N	D

Broom

Cytisus scoparius

ID FACT FILE

Height: 1–3 m

Flowers: Golden yellow, 15–25 mm long, in short, dense clusters

Leaves: On young shoots only, each with 3 spear-shaped or narrowly oval, silky-hairy leaflets

Fruits: Flattened pods, 25–40 mm long, hairy on the margins

Lookalikes: Gorse (p.74) is spiny, with shorter pods. Spanish Broom (*Spartium junceum*), escaping from gardens mostly on to railway embankments, has larger flowers in long, loose clusters.

An erect shrub, the stems 5-angled and apparently leafless. A locally common plant of open woods, heaths, cliffs, shingle beaches, dry banks and disused railway tracks. The stems were formerly important for fodder and bedding and were cut and sold in bundles for brooms. Broom and Gorse (p.74) were part of the rural economy of heathland, a habitat that is notably characteristic of parts of Britain. A prostrate variant of Broom is sometimes found on cliffs in Cornwall, Wales and Ireland and on coastal shingle in Kent.

J	F	M	A	M	J
J	A	S	O	N	D

Tufted Vetch

Vicia cracca

ID FACT FILE

Height: 50–200cm

Flowers: Bluish-purple, 8–15 mm long, in dense, 1-sided clusters of 10–40 atop a long stalk

Leaves: Compound, with 6–15 pairs of oblong or narrowly oval leaflets and a long, branched terminal tendril

Fruits: Flattened, brown, hairless pods 10–22 mm long

Lookalikes: Other vetches, but distinguished by the larger clusters of bluish-purple flowers.

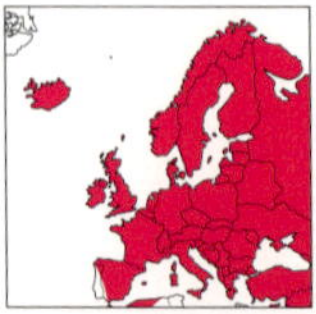

Rather hairy perennial, scrambling by means of tendrils, of bushy and grassy places, especially hedgerows, scrub and woodland margins, and old meadows. This striking flower of summer is perhaps the most familiar of the several native vetches. It is rarely seen in meadows today because of their destruction by modern agriculture. Some plants are very hairy. Tufted Vetch belongs to a group of five closely related European species that can be very difficult to tell apart.

J	F	M	A	M	J
J	A	S	O	N	D

Bush Vetch

Vicia sepium

ID FACT FILE

Height: 20–100 cm

Flowers: Pale bluish-purple, rarely lilac or cream, 10–15 mm long, in clusters of 2–6 on a short stalk

Leaves: Compound, with 3–9 pairs of oblong or oval leaflets and a branched terminal tendril

Fruits: Flattened, black, beaked, hairless pods 20–35 mm long

Lookalikes: Other vetches, but distinguished by the small clusters of dull bluish-purple flowers.

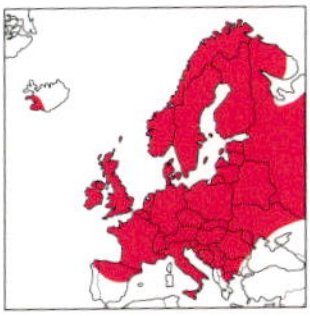

A downy, scrambling, trailing or climbing perennial that is a common plant of roadsides, hedgerows, scrub and open woods. The plant spreads by underground runners to form large patches. The flowers have a slightly faded, dowdy appearance by contrast with the bright colours of our other native vetches. A remarkable dwarf and compact variant, with few or no leaf-tendrils, occurs here and there on sand-dunes in remote parts of N and W Scotland and NW Ireland.

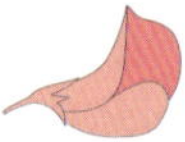

J	F	M	A	M	J
J	A	S	O	N	D

Common Vetch

Vicia sativa

ID FACT FILE

Height: 20–120 cm

Flowers: Bright pink, purplish-crimson or purple, 10–15 mm long, stalkless, solitary or in pairs

Leaves: Compound, with 3–8 pairs of oblong or oval, very narrow to almost heart-shaped leaflets and a branched terminal tendril

Fruits: Black or yellowish-brown, hairless or downy pods 25–70 mm long

Lookalikes: Other vetches, but distinguished by the combination of leaf-tendrils and solitary or paired pinkish flowers.

A hairy, climbing or trailing perennial, often rather neat in habit by comparison with other vetches, growing in grassy places, borders of fields, waysides and hedge-banks, in many places as a relic of former cultivation for fodder. A very variable species which has been divided by botanists into several subspecies. The variation partly reflects a long history as a crop, with much seed being brought in from abroad. Plants with bright pink flowers and narrow leaflets are probably native.

J	F	M	A	M	J
J	A	S	O	N	D

Meadow, or Yellow, Vetchling

Lathyrus pratensis

ID FACT FILE

Height: 30–120 cm

Flowers: Yellow, 12–20 mm long, in clusters of 5–12 atop a long, erect stalk

Leaves: Paired, spear-shaped, entire leaflets up to 5 cm long, with a pair of large, leaflet-like structures at the base and a branched terminal tendril

Fruits: Black, hairless pods 2–4 cm long

Lookalikes: Bird's-foot Trefoil (p.86) has no tendrils, leaflets in fives and smaller, often orange-tinted, flowers.

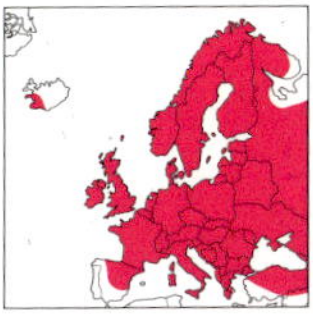

Climbing or sprawling perennial, arising from a slender rhizome, with angled, square, slightly winged, rather weak, leafy stems. It is common and conspicuous in grassy places, marshes, hedge-banks, scrub and woodland margins; indeed, it is one of the most familiar and attractive of all our grassland wild flowers. It is a principal food plant for the caterpillar of the Wood White butterfly. An infusion of this plant has been used as a remedy for coughs and bronchitis.

J	F	M	A	M	J
J	A	S	O	N	D

Tall, or Golden, Melilot

Melilotus altissimus

ID FACT FILE

Height: 50–150 cm

Flowers: Yellow, 5–7 mm long, in loose, 1-sided, many-flowered clusters; the petals are all the same length

Leaves: Leaflets 3, wedge-shaped or oval, toothed

Fruits: Black, short-hairy pods 3–5 mm long

Lookalikes: Common Melilot (*Melilotus officinalis*) is often taller, with the upper 3 petals longer than the lower pair, and the fruit brown and hairless; White Melilot (*Melilotus alba*) has white flowers.

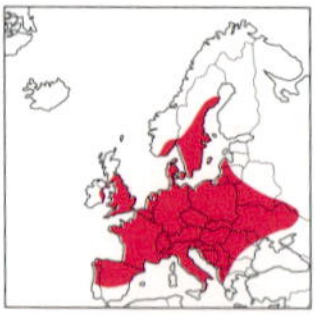

An erect, branched, often quite robust annual, biennial or short-lived perennial that is widespread on waste ground, field borders and agricultural land. It tends to prefer heavier soils. It may be native, but has been spread by cultivation as a fodder crop; it has also been used medicinally and may have been first introduced here by 16th-century herbalists. It is rare in Scotland, and in Ireland it occurs only near the coasts of Co. Dublin and Co. Wicklow.

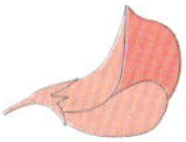

J	F	M	A	M	J
J	A	S	O	N	D

Common Restharrow

Ononis repens

ID FACT FILE

Height: 10–70 cm

Flowers: Purplish-pink, 15–20 mm long, in loose, leafy clusters

Leaves: Leaflets 1 or 3, wedge-shaped or oval, toothed, densely sticky-hairy

Fruits: Pods 5–7 mm long, enclosed within the calyx

Lookalikes: Spiny Restharrow (*Ononis spinosa*) is more erect and spiny; it is much less common and does not occur in Ireland.

A sticky-hairy, spreading perennial, forming patches in dry grassland and on sand-dunes, shingle beaches and other habitats on well-drained, usually lime-rich soils. It is a widespread plant, although less common in much of Scotland and W Ireland. The plant sometimes has a few soft spines. The tough roots and stems were a nuisance to farmers before mechanised ploughing, and the foliage is said to have tainted the milk of cattle that fed on it.

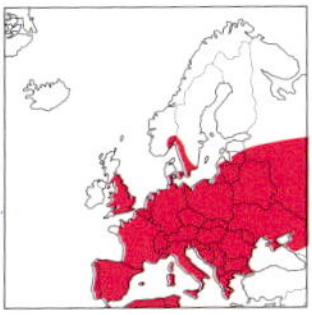

J	F	M	A	M	J
J	A	S	O	N	D

Black Medick

Medicago lupulina

ID FACT FILE

Height: 5–60 cm

Flowers: Tiny, golden yellow, up to 50 in spherical heads 3–9 mm across, on a long stalk

Leaves: Leaflets 3, oval or almost circular, blunt and notched at tip, the middle one stalked

Fruits: Pods 2–3 mm long, 1-seeded, kidney-shaped, black

Lookalikes: The black pods are distinctive; Lesser Trefoil (p.83) is a more slender, hairless plant with petals persisting in fruit.

Often rather hairy, sometimes even slightly sticky-hairy, prostrate or weakly erect annual, or short-lived perennial, of dry grassland, sunny banks, walls, waysides, coastal cliffs and sand-dunes. It is common throughout, but less so in Scotland. Many plants of waste places and fields are more robust and more erect; they probably derive from former cultivation as a fodder crop or from the use of commercial, non-native wild flower seed. This plant is often confused with three native yellow-flowered clovers.

J	F	M	A	M	J
J	A	S	O	N	D

Lesser Trefoil or Suckling Clover

Trifolium dubium

ID FACT FILE

HEIGHT: 10–30 cm, sometimes up to 50 cm

FLOWERS: Tiny, yellow, 10–20 in spherical heads 7–9 mm across, on a long stalk

LEAVES: Leaflets 3, oval, toothed, the middle one stalked

FRUITS: Tiny, inconspicuous, 1-seeded pods enclosed within persistent corolla

LOOKALIKES: Black Medick (p.82) is a more robust, somewhat hairy plant with denser heads and conspicuous black fruits; the petals do not persist in fruit.

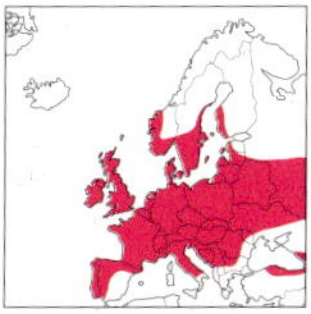

Prostrate or ascending annual of dry grassland, sand-dunes, walls, rocky ground and sometimes cultivated land. This is the commonest of the several native annual clovers, all of them plants of open, dry grassland, often near the sea. It prefers well-drained soils and in old grassland frequently grows on ant-hills. This plant has by far the strongest claim of all the clovers to be the 'true' *Seamróge* or Shamrock of Ireland (*see* Wood Sorrel, p.89) and is widely sold as such for St Patrick's Day on 17 March.

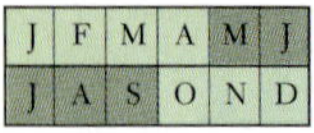

Red Clover

Trifolium pratense

ID FACT FILE

Height: 20–60 cm, sometimes up to 100 cm

Flowers: Pale or dark pink, or reddish-purple, rarely white, 12–15 mm long, in dense, solitary or paired, almost spherical heads 2–4 cm long, with 2 leaves immediately below

Leaves: Leaflets 3, oval or almost circular, hairy beneath, often marked with a whitish crescent

Fruits: Inconspicuous, 1-seeded pods enclosed within persistent corolla; the fruiting head is a brown ball of dead flowers

Lookalikes: The commonest red-flowered clover.

A rather hairy, tufted, sprawling, ascending or erect, short-lived perennial of grasslands, waysides and waste ground throughout Britain and Ireland. A very variable species. Many plants derive from introduced fodder crops or wild flower seed: these are robust, tall and erect, and have large, often pale pink heads of flowers, whereas the true native plant has a more prostrate or sprawling habit and smaller heads of usually richly red or reddish-purple flowers. The flowers are much visited by bumblebees.

J	F	M	A	M	J
J	A	S	O	N	D

White, or Dutch, Clover

Trifolium repens

ID FACT FILE

Height: 20–50 cm

Flowers: Scented, white, often tinged pink, 8–13 mm long, in dense, solitary, long-stalked, spherical heads 1–3 cm across

Leaves: Long-stalked; leaflets 3, oval or almost circular, each frequently marked with a whitish V or dark markings

Fruits: Inconspicuous, 1- to 4-seeded pods, enclosed within persistent corolla; the fruiting head is a brown ball of dead flowers

Lookalikes: The common white-flowered clover of grassland in Britain and Ireland.

A creeping perennial, with rooting, prostrate stems, forming large patches in lawns, grasslands, waysides and waste ground throughout Britain and Ireland. A variable species, with most plants probably now derived from cultivated stocks. White Clover is of considerable economic value as a fodder crop and source of nectar for bees; bacteria in nodules on the roots convert atmospheric nitrogen to usable plant nutrients. A special variety with purple flowers occurs in the Isles of Scilly.

J	F	M	A	M	J
J	A	S	O	N	D

Bird's-foot Trefoil

Lotus corniculatus

ID FACT FILE

Height: 5–50 cm

Flowers: Yellow, often streaked or tinted orange or red, 10–18 mm long, 3–8 in clusters atop a long stalk

Leaves: Each with 5 spear-shaped to almost circular leaflets

Fruits: Cylindrical pods 10–15 mm long, arranged like a bird's foot

Lookalikes: Marsh Bird's-foot Trefoil (*Lotus uliginosus*) is taller and hairier, with calyx-teeth in bud spreading at right-angles. Meadow Vetchling (p.79) has tendrils and larger, entirely yellow flowers.

A prostrate, sprawling or erect perennial, forming patches; widespread in dry grassland and on sunny banks, cliffs, rocks and sand-dunes, even lawns, throughout Britain and Ireland. It grows on well-drained soils, particularly those derived from sand or limestone. On road-verges and elsewhere plants are often more robust and erect (Fodder Bird's-foot Trefoil), and are a non-native variety derived from commercial wild flower seed. It is an important food plant for caterpillars of Blue and other butterflies.

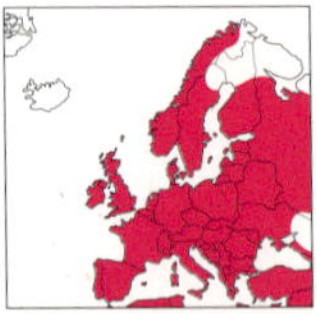

J	F	M	A	M	J
J	A	S	O	N	D

Kidney Vetch

Anthyllis vulneraria

ID FACT FILE

Height: 10–50 cm

Flowers: Usually yellow, 12–15 mm long, in dense, paired heads 2–4 cm across, with 2 deeply divided bracts immediately below; calyx inflated, hairy, usually red-tipped

Leaves: Leaflets 3–9, oval or oblong, silky-hairy beneath, the terminal one larger, especially on lower leaves

Fruits: Egg-shaped, flattened, 1-seeded pods, enclosed within persistent calyx

Lookalikes: The 2 deeply divided bracts below the paired flower-heads distinguish this plant from other pea flowers.

A handsome, prostrate, ascending or erect biennial or short-lived perennial of grasslands and rocky ground, especially on coastal cliffs and sand-dunes and on dry, lime-rich soils inland. Dry banks by the sea are sometimes covered with this plant and in some areas, such as Cornwall and Co. Cork, the colour of the flowers can vary from shades of yellow through cream to pink, red and purple. Tall, erect plants on road-verges usually derive from wild flower seed imported from C Europe.

J	F	M	A	M	J
J	A	S	O	N	D

Sainfoin

Onobrychis viciifola

ID FACT FILE

Height: 20–100 cm

Flowers: Rich pink, with purplish veins, 10–14 mm long, in long, dense spikes up to 9 cm long

Leaves: Compound, with 6–14 pairs of oval or oblong leaflets

Fruits: 1-seeded, oval, flattened, strongly veined and toothed pods, 5–8 mm long

Lookalikes: Red-flowered clovers have leaves with 3 leaflets, egg-shaped or spherical flower-heads and inconspicuous fruits.

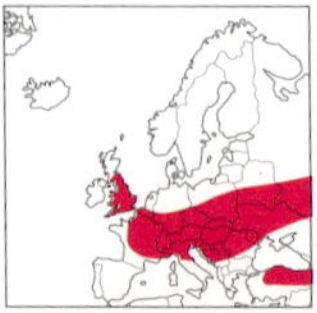

A clump-forming perennial arising from a woody root; locally common in limestone grassland and on road-verges. One of Britain's most showy wild plants, it has a distinctly exotic feel. However, it is certainly native on the chalk of S England – and is mentioned in John Gerard's famous 1597 *Herball* – although many plants today probably derive from its former use as a fodder crop; and it is now an important component of wild flower seed-mixtures. It is absent from Ireland.

J	F	M	A	M	J
J	A	S	O	N	D

Wood Sorrel

Oxalis acetosella

ID FACT FILE

Height: 10–20 cm

Flowers: Solitary on almost leafless stems, bell-shaped, nodding, 8–15 mm long, white with lilac veins or sometimes all lilac

Leaves: Long-stalked, delicate, pale green, often purplish beneath; leaflets 3, heart-shaped, notched

Fruits: Egg-shaped, 5-angled capsules, exploding when ripe to disperse the seeds

Lookalikes: Pink Sorrel (*Oxalis articulata*), with clusters of bright pink flowers, is a garden escape on roadsides and waste ground.

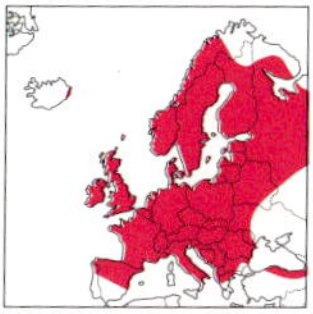

Delicate, slender, hairless perennial, with creeping rhizome, clothed in swollen, scale-like remains of leaf-bases; widespread in moist, shady woods and on mountain-ledges. The leaves have a sharp acid taste and were formerly used as a flavouring, like those of Sorrel (p.17). This plant has some claim to be the *Seamróge* or Shamrock by which St Patrick illustrated the concept of the Holy Trinity to the then pagan Irish; however that is more likely to have been Lesser Trefoil (p.83).

J	F	M	A	M	J
J	A	S	O	N	D

Meadow Cranesbill

Geranium pratense

ID FACT FILE

HEIGHT: 30–80 cm

FLOWERS: Cup-shaped, bluish-violet, 25–40 cm across, in rather compact terminal clusters; 5 petals, without notches

LEAVES: Cut into 5–7 deeply lobed, oblong, toothed segments

FRUITS: Hairy, beak-like, with 5 segments that curl upwards explosively when ripe to disperse the seed

LOOKALIKES: Bloody Cranesbill (*Geranium sanguineum*), with solitary reddish-purple flowers and notched petals, occurs on limestone, often by the sea, notably the Burren of Co. Clare.

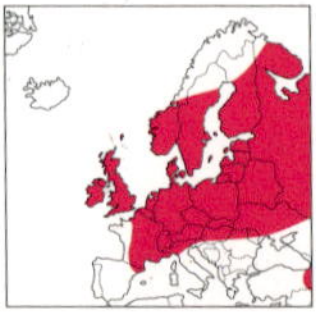

Robust and handsome perennial, arising from a woody root and somewhat sticky in upper part; locally common in grassy places, roadsides, scrub and woodland margins over most of Britain except N Scotland; introduced in Cornwall. It can be locally abundant. In Ireland it is restricted to the coast of Co. Antrim, although here and there elsewhere it is a garden escape. The flower-stalks, down-curved after flowering, are erect in fruit.

J	F	M	A	M	J
J	A	S	O	N	D

Dove's-foot Cranesbill

Geranium molle

A hairy, branched, weak-stemmed annual of disturbed and open ground, especially waysides, waste ground and coastal sand-dunes, and even dry, unmanicured lawns. This is the commonest of a group of small, rather similar annual or short-lived perennial cranesbills, all plants of ground opened up by human activity. They are characterised by round, deeply lobed or dissected leaves, small, pink or purplish flowers and long, slender, beak-like fruits.

ID FACT FILE

Height: 5–40 cm

Flowers: Dish-shaped, purplish-pink or rarely white, 5–10 mm across, in very loose terminal clusters; 5 deeply notched petals

Leaves: Deeply divided into 3–5 3-lobed segments, softly hairy, slightly greyish-green

Fruits: Slightly wrinkled, hairless, beak-like, with 5 segments that curl upwards explosively when ripe to disperse the seed

Lookalikes: The commonest of several annual cranesbills that occur in Britain and Ireland.

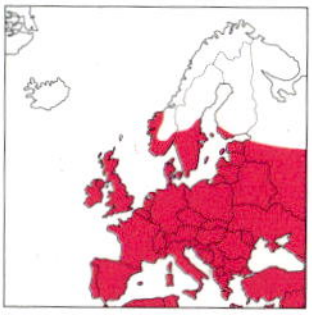

J	F	M	A	M	J
J	A	S	O	N	D

Herb Robert

Geranium robertianum

ID FACT FILE

Height: 20–50 cm

Flowers: Dish-shaped, purplish-pink, 15–30 mm across, in very loose terminal clusters; 5 petals; stamens usually orange

Leaves: Rather fern-like, cut almost to the base into 3–5 deeply lobed segments

Fruits: Slightly wrinkled, beak-like, with 5 segments that curl upwards explosively when ripe to disperse the seed

Lookalikes: Several plants in the carrot family have similar fern-like leaves, but very different flowers.

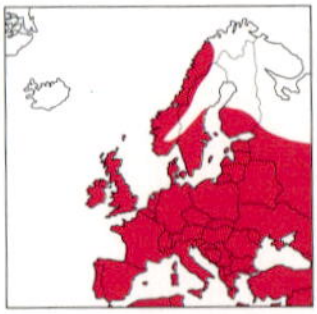

Rather dainty, aromatic, reddish, hairy, annual, biennial or short-lived perennial with straggling, brittle, fleshy stems. It is a common plant of shady places, cliffs, rocks, walls and coastal shingle beaches; and a weed of shady gardens and old glasshouses. Plants from W Britain and Ireland sometimes have white flowers. A small-flowered subspecies of Herb Robert (known as Little Robin), with yellow stamens and more wrinkled fruits, is a choice rarity of S and W England and Co. Cork.

J	F	M	A	M	J
J	A	S	O	N	D

Common Stork's-bill

Erodium cicutarium

ID FACT FILE

Height: 5–60 cm

Flowers: Dish-shaped, purplish-pink, lilac or sometimes white, 8–20 mm across, 2–12 in loose heads; 5 deeply notched petals

Leaves: Almost fern-like, divided twice into deeply lobed segments, softly hairy or sticky-hairy

Fruits: Slightly wrinkled, with a beak up to 6 cm long and 5 segments that twist explosively into spirals when ripe

Lookalikes: The cranesbills lack the spiral twisting of the fruit-segments; apart from Herb Robert (p.92), they do not have fern-like leaves.

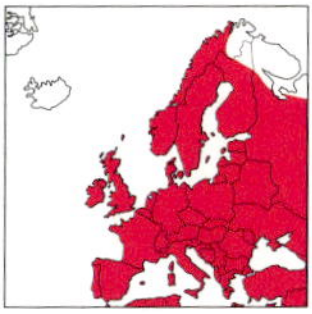

Hairy annual, biennial or short-lived perennial, of open sandy and stony ground and thin grassland, especially by the sea; a very common plant on sand-dunes, where it is mostly prostrate and can be sticky-hairy. It is mainly coastal in Ireland. The explosive release of the seeds serves to disperse them efficiently; each has a spiral, corkscrew-like segment of the fruit wall attached, which screws it into loose soil. A variable species, notably in the colour and size of the petals.

J	F	M	A	M	J
J	A	S	O	N	D

Dog's Mercury

Mercurialis perennis

ID FACT FILE

Height: 20–50 cm

Flowers: 4–5 mm across, green, with 3 sepals, the male ones in erect tassel-like clusters, the female ones in clusters of 2–3

Leaves: In opposite pairs, elliptical, neatly toothed on the margins, dark green, pointed

Fruits: 2-lobed, hairy capsules 6–8 mm long

Lookalikes: Annual Mercury (*Mercurialis annua*) is a pale green, hairless annual of cultivated and waste land in S England and S and E Ireland.

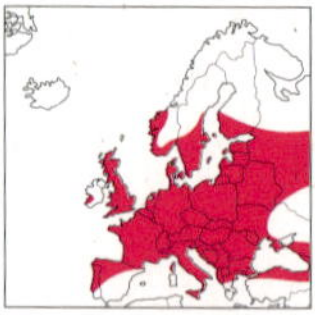

Hairy perennial with a branched rhizome, forming extensive patches in woodland and shady hedge-banks. It is a characteristic plant of ancient woodlands, but spreads into hedges. It is very rare in Ireland, where, apart from possibly native plants on limestone in Co. Clare, it has been introduced into a few planted woodland estates. The common name refers to the poisonous nature of this plant. Flowers are either male or female, each on separate plants, and the catkin-like flowers are wind-pollinated.

J	F	M	A	M	J
J	A	S	O	N	D

Wood Spurge

Euphorbia amygdaloides

ID FACT FILE

Height: 20–80 cm

Flowers: Yellowish, with complex structure characteristic of the spurges: a cluster of tiny male and female flowers within an envelope or involucre

Leaves: Spear-shaped, oblong or somewhat spoon-shaped, up to 8 cm long

Fruits: 3-celled, pitted and grooved capsules 3–4 mm long

Lookalikes: The only perennial (and common) spurge of woodlands.

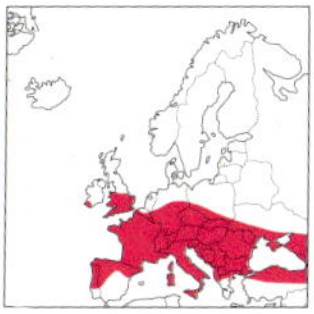

A striking, clump-forming, erect, hairy, often reddish or purplish-tinged perennial of open woods and coppices. It is a distinctive plant of the oak and beech woodlands of S England, extending to N Wales; in the Isles of Scilly it occurs in open heathland by the sea. In Ireland it occurs only in Co. Cork; absent from Scotland. The cut stems and leaves exude a poisonous, white juice. One of the cultivated garden spurges (*Euphorbia robbii*), originally collected in NW Turkey, is now regarded as a subspecies of this plant.

J	F	M	A	M	J
J	A	S	O	N	D

Sun Spurge

Euphorbia helioscopa

ID FACT FILE

Height: 10–50 cm

Flowers: Yellowish, with complex structure characteristic of the spurges: a cluster of tiny male and female flowers within an envelope or involucre

Leaves: Oval or spoon-shaped, toothed towards the tip

Fruits: Smooth capsules 2–3.5 mm long

Lookalikes: Petty Spurge (*Euphorbia peplus*), a branched, leafy annual with untoothed leaves, is more a weed of gardens.

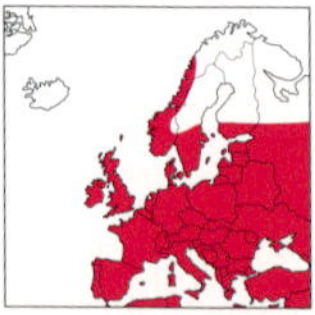

An erect, mostly unbranched, yellowish-green, hairless annual of disturbed and cultivated ground, especially arable land. This plant grows best on rich soils and accumulates the mineral nutrient boron. The cut stems and leaves exude a poisonous, white juice, which was a traditional remedy for warts. There are some 15 spurges in Britain and Ireland, several of them rare. This and Petty Spurge (*see* LOOKALIKES) are the only common spurges of cultivated land.

J	F	M	A	M	J
J	A	S	O	N	D

Common Milkwort

Polygala vulgaris

ID FACT FILE

Height: 10–35 cm

Flowers: 4–7 mm long, with 5 petal-like sepals and a tiny corolla, mostly blue but also magenta, lilac, pink, white or white flushed with blue; 10–40 in loose, erect clusters

Leaves: Unpaired, narrowly elliptical, the lower ones smaller than the upper

Fruits: Flattened, egg-shaped capsules c.5 mm long, enclosed within the green, persistent calyx

Lookalikes: Heath Milkwort (*Polygala serpyllifolia*), of acid grassland, has at least the lowest leaves in opposite pairs.

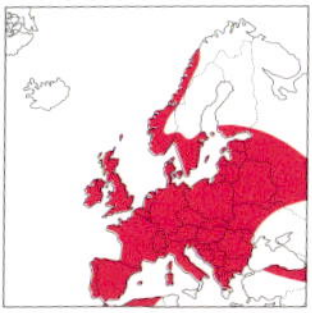

Slender, prostrate, sprawling or weakly ascending perennial; widespread in dry grassland, especially on chalk or limestone soils, and on sand-dunes and cliffs. The flowers, which are intricate in structure, are variable in colour even within a small area. This is the commonest of five native species of milkwort. Milkworts were prescribed by herbalists to nursing mothers and were once a feature of garlands for Rogation or 'beating the bounds' rituals.

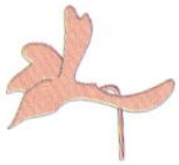

J	F	M	A	M	J
J	A	S	O	N	D

Himalayan Balsam or Policeman's Helmet

Impatiens glandulifera

ID FACT FILE

Height: 1–3 m

Flowers: In loose clusters, 25–40 mm long, purplish-pink, pink or white; 5 fused petals and 3 sepals, the largest a spurred bag

Leaves: In opposite pairs or threes, spear-shaped or elliptical, pointed, with red-toothed margins

Fruits: Fleshy, cylindrical capsules that explode to scatter the black seeds

Lookalikes: Other balsams have yellow or orange flowers.

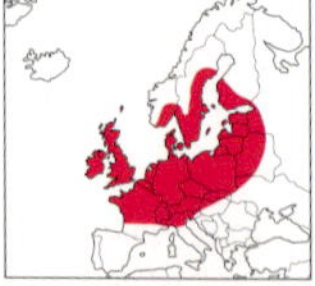

Impressive, hairless annual, with stout, brittle, juicy, often reddish stems with knobbly joints, and a sickly-sweet aromatic smell. It is a widespread and conspicuous feature of late summer on riverbanks, streamsides and in damp and shady waste places, often in huge crowds. A native of the Himalayas, it was introduced to gardens in the mid-19th century and has since spread rapidly in Britain and Ireland, aided by the violent seed dispersal mechanism. The flowers are much visited by bumblebees.

J	F	M	A	M	J
J	A	S	O	N	D

Common Mallow

Malva sylvestris

ID FACT FILE

Height: 20–100 cm, sometimes up to 150 cm

Flowers: 2–4 cm across, pinkish-purple or lilac, with darker veins, with 5 deeply notched petals

Leaves: Long-stalked, kidney- to heart-shaped or almost circular, with 3–7 toothed lobes; often with a dark blotch

Fruits: Disc-shaped whorl of 1-seeded nutlets

Lookalikes: Musk Mallow (p.100) has deeply cut leaves and pale pink or white flowers; Dwarf Mallow (*Malva neglecta*) is smaller and usually prostrate, with pale lilac flowers.

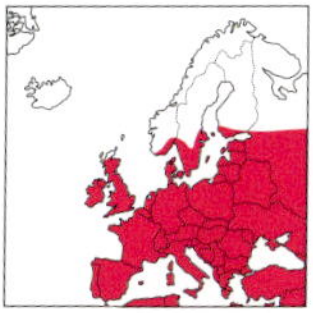

Prostrate, sprawling or erect, softly hairy biennial, or short-lived perennial, of waste places, roadsides, dry and disturbed grassland and hedge-banks. The plant adds colour to even the scruffiest roadside. The leaves have soothing medicinal properties and have traditionally been a source of winter greens in Europe and elsewhere; they are still made into a soup in parts of the Mediterranean region. The edible fruits have long been known by children in country districts as 'cheeses'.

J	F	M	A	M	J
J	A	S	O	N	D

Musk Mallow

Malva moschata

ID FACT FILE

Height: 30–80 cm

Flowers: 25–50 mm across, pale pink or white, smelling of musk, with 5 notched petals

Leaves: Lower leaves rounded, but others deeply cut into strap-shaped segments

Fruits: Disc-shaped whorl of hairy, 1-seeded nutlets

Lookalikes: Common Mallow (p.99) and Dwarf Mallow (*Malva neglecta*), which has flowers less than 25 mm across, have shallowly lobed leaves.

Elegant, erect, little-branched perennial with hairy stems, of grassland and hedge-banks. It is a widespread but often rather local plant that extends northwards to S Scotland, although it is mostly restricted in Ireland to the south-east. Like other mallows, it was used in cough medicines on account of the soothing properties of the sap. It has long been grown in cottage gardens and is a popular component of wildflower seed mixtures.

J	F	M	A	M	J
J	A	S	O	N	D

Common, or Perforate, St John's Wort

Hypericum perforatum

ID FACT FILE

Height:
30–100 cm

Flowers:
10–15 mm across, yellow, in branched clusters; 5 petals, twisted and reddish in bud; 5 sepals, each with a few black dots; many yellow stamens

Leaves: In opposite pairs, 1–2 cm long, oblong or oval, with many translucent dots

Fruits: Pear-shaped capsules, 4–6 mm, splitting into 3 segments

Lookalikes: Slender St John's Wort (*Hypericum pulchrum*), a dainty plant up to 40 cm tall, with reddish petals, occurs on heaths.

Erect, hairless perennial of dry grasslands, scrub, woodland margins and waste ground; it is the commonest of the dozen or so native species of St John's wort, but rare in N Scotland. It was associated with Christian and pagan Summer Solstice festivals (St John's Day is 24 June) and was thought to ward off witchcraft and spells. It is poisonous to stock, making their skin sensitive to sunlight. It is a troublesome weed in N America, where it has been introduced.

J	F	M	A	M	J
J	A	S	O	N	D

In winter in milder districts.

Sweet Violet

Viola odorata

ID FACT FILE

Height: 5–20 cm

Flowers: 12–15 mm long, richly scented, usually white, but also purplish-violet, reddish-purple, pink or lilac, solitary on leafless stems

Leaves: Long-stalked in a rosette, heart-shaped, downy

Fruits: Pointed capsules, splitting into 3 segments

Lookalikes: Dog Violet (p.103) has hairless leaves and bluish-violet, unscented flowers borne on leafy stems.

A dainty, tufted perennial of hedge-banks, scrub and woodland. One of the best-loved and most welcome flowers of early spring, it has long been grown in gardens; its natural distribution has thus been obscured and it frequently grows not far from houses. White is the commonest flower colour amongst wild plants. In summer the leaves enlarge greatly to make the most of the reduced light in woodland. The plant reproduces both by seeds, dispersed by ants, and by long, rooting runners.

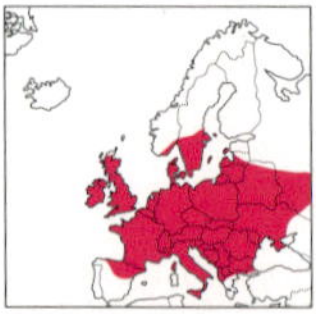

J	F	M	A	M	J
J	A	S	O	N	D

Dog-violet

Viola riviniana

ID FACT FILE

Height: 5–20 cm

Flowers: 15–25 mm long, bluish-violet, with a pale spur, solitary on leafy stems

Leaves: Long-stalked, heart-shaped, hairless

Fruits: Pointed capsules, splitting into 3 segments

Lookalikes: Early Dog-violet (*Viola reichenbachiana*), mainly in S England, has smaller, all-violet flowers. Sweet Violet (p.102) has white, purplish or violet, scented flowers.

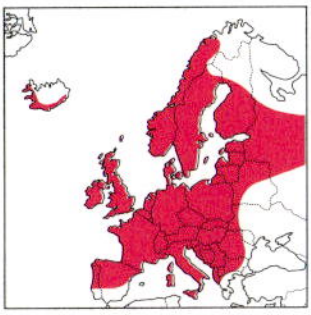

A tufted perennial of hedge-banks, scrub, woodland, grassland, mountain ledges and coastal heaths. It can spread rapidly to become quite a persistent weed in gardens. Like all violets and pansies the flowers hang upside-down, as the flower-stalk bends sharply just below the flower. The largest petal is produced into a spur or sac. The seeds are dispersed by ants. There are several closely related dog-violets, which cross with one another to form a confusing range of hybrids.

J	F	M	A	M	J
J	A	S	O	N	D

Field Pansy

Viola arvensis

ID FACT FILE

Height: 5–40 cm

Flowers: 10–18 mm long, cream, variably marked with yellow and bluish-violet, solitary on leafy stems; petals shorter than the sepals

Leaves: Oblong or spoon-shaped, lobed or toothed

Fruits: Pointed capsules, splitting into 3 segments

Lookalikes: Wild Pansy or Heartsease (*Viola tricolor*) has larger, violet, purple or yellow flowers, the petals longer than the sepals.

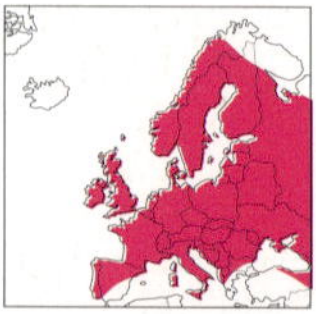

An annual with weak, ascending stems; often abundant on cultivated land and one of the few weeds of arable land to have persisted in the face of modern chemical sprays. It is still widespread, except in N Scotland, and locally common in cereal crops. It is a very variable species that crosses with other wild pansies (see Lookalikes) to produce a complex array of forms; several of these variants have been described as species, subspecies and varieties.

J	F	M	A	M	J
J	A	S	O	N	D

Rock-rose

Helianthemum nummularium

ID FACT FILE

HEIGHT: 10–40 cm

FLOWERS: 18–25 mm across, yellow, in few-flowered clusters, with 5 prominently veined sepals, 5 flimsy petals and many stamens

LEAVES: Narrow, oblong, 1-veined, white-hairy beneath

FRUITS: Egg-shaped capsules, splitting into 3 segments

LOOKALIKES: Hoary Rock-rose (*Helianthemum canum*), with narrower leaves and smaller flowers 10–15 mm across, occurs in N England, the coasts of SW and N Wales and the Burren of Co. Clare, Ireland.

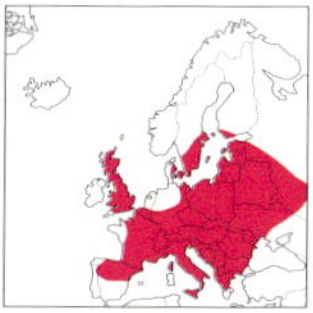

Straggling, branched shrublet, often very woody at the base. Widespread in Britain, except Cornwall and parts of Scotland, in chalk grassland and grassy and rocky places on limestone and basalt, but absent from Ireland except for one station on the coast of Co. Donegal. In the Burren of Co. Clare, this species is replaced by the smaller-flowered Hoary Rock-rose (see LOOKALIKES). Britain's three native rock-roses are a fragment of an important family of Mediterranean shrubs that includes the sun-roses (*Cistus*).

J	F	M	A	M	J
J	A	S	O	N	D

White Bryony

Bryonia cretica

Bristly, climbing or trailing perennial, arising from a stout, tuberous rhizome, growing in hedges and scrub and on woodland margins. The great root, thought fancifully to resemble a human body, has in the past been called Mandrake – and was once sold as such. (The true plant of that name grows in the Mediterranean region.) White Bryony is rarer in N and W Britain and rare in Ireland, introduced to a few sites in Ulster and near Dublin. The plant is poisonous.

ID FACT FILE

Height: 1–4 m

Flowers: Greenish-white with darker veins, in stalked clusters, the male and female on different plants

Leaves: 5- or 7-lobed, like a large ivy leaf; long, spirally twisted tendrils opposite leaves

Fruits: Spherical red berries up to 1 cm across

Lookalikes: Black Bryony (p.242), another climbing plant of hedges, has hairless, heart-shaped leaves. Hop (p.11) has cone- or tassel-like flowers.

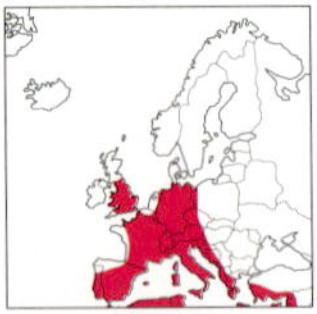

J	F	M	A	M	J
J	A	S	O	N	D

Purple Loosestrife

Lythrum salicaria

ID FACT FILE

Height: 50–180 cm

Flowers: 1 cm, reddish-purple, with 6 (sometimes 4) petals, in whorls, massed in long, dense spikes

Leaves: In opposite pairs or threes, spear-shaped or oval, clasping the stem slightly

Fruits: Egg-shaped capsules, 3–4 mm, with many tiny seeds

Lookalikes: Rosebay Willowherb (p.110) has larger, 4-petalled flowers and grows in drier places.

Striking, erect, short-hairy perennial, with 4-angled stems, forming prominent clumps in marshes, beside rivers and streams, and on damp waste ground. In W Ireland especially it provides bold splashes of colour to the landscape during late summer, even away from water. Three types of flower are produced, on different plants, each with stigmas of different length; this modification enhances cross-pollination by insects. The sticky seeds are dispersed on the feet and feathers of waterfowl.

J	F	M	A	M	J
J	A	S	O	N	D

Enchanter's Nightshade

Circaea lutetiana

ID FACT FILE

Height: 10–50 cm

Flowers: 5–8 mm across, white or pink, in loose, leafless spikes that elongate as flowers open; 4 petals, 2 deeply notched

Leaves: In opposite pairs, heart-shaped or broadly oval, shallowly toothed; stalk unwinged (see Lookalikes)

Fruits: Pear-shaped, 2-seeded, covered with minute, hooked bristles

Lookalikes: Alpine Enchanter's Nightshade (*Circaea alpina*) has leaves with winged stalks and the flower-spike elongates after flowering.

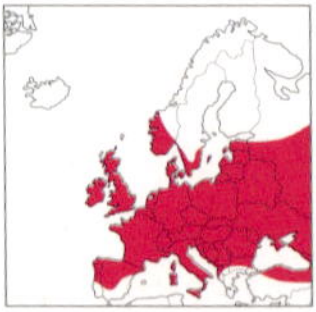

A sparsely downy perennial of woods, shady lanes and shady gardens, where it can be a weed. It spreads both by runners and by seed and sometimes occurs in large numbers. The bristles on the fruits adhere to fur and clothes and serve to disperse the seeds. It is replaced locally by Alpine Enchanter's Nightshade (see Lookalikes); also, many plants in Wales, N Britain and N Ireland are intermediate between the two species and appear to be hybrids between them.

J	F	M	A	M	J
J	A	S	O	N	D

Evening Primrose

Oenothera biennis

ID FACT FILE

Height: 80–150 cm

Flowers: 4–6 cm across, with 4 pale yellow petals and green sepals, in a long, erect cluster

Leaves: Short-stalked, narrow, broadly spear-shaped, shallowly toothed

Fruits: Slender, downy capsules c.3 cm long

Lookalikes: Large-flowered Evening Primrose (*Oenothera erythrosepala*) has hairs with red, swollen bases and flowers 5–8 cm across, with reddish sepals.

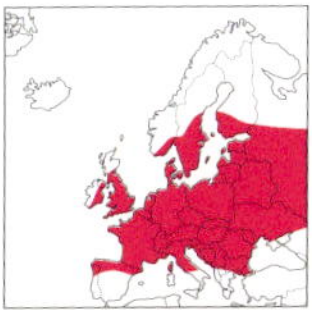

Erect annual, or biennial, with downy stems; locally common on roadsides and other open, sandy ground, waste places and gardens. The roots are edible and the plant is increasingly being grown for its oil, which is used in cosmetic and medical products. Although introduced from N America, this plant has become a familiar, established member of the British flora; it is rarer in the north and in Wales. The flowers open in the evening and are pollinated by night-flying moths.

WILLOWHERB AND EVENING PRIMROSE FAMILY, ONAGRACEAE

J	F	M	A	M	J
J	A	S	O	N	D

Rosebay Willowherb or Fireweed

Chamerion angustifolium

ID FACT FILE

Height: 80–250 cm

Flowers: c.25 mm across, with 4 purplish-pink petals; in long, loose, tapering spikes; buds down-turned

Leaves: Alternate, short-stalked, narrow, spear-shaped

Fruits: Slender capsules, up to 6 cm long, splitting to release the numerous seeds, each with a plume of silky hairs

Lookalikes: Purple Loosestrife (p.107) has smaller, usually 6-petalled flowers and grows in wet places.

Erect, almost hairless perennial, with creeping rhizomes, forming extensive patches; a very common and conspicuous plant of woodland clearings, heathland, waste ground and derelict industrial land, railway embankments and sand-dunes. This species has expanded its range greatly during the present century, especially since World War II, when it spread rapidly in the ruins of bombed buildings. However, it remains uncommon over much of Ireland. The hairy seeds are dispersed by the wind.

J	F	M	A	M	J
J	A	S	O	N	D

Great Hairy Willowherb or Codlins-and-Cream

Epilobium hirsutum

ID FACT FILE

Height: 1–2 m

Flowers: 20–25 mm across, in loose clusters, with 4 purplish-pink or occasionally white, shallowly notched petals, and a prominent, 4-lobed stigma; buds erect

Leaves: Opposite, half-clasping the stem, oblong or spear-shaped, shallowly toothed

Fruits: Slender, downy capsules, 4–8 cm long, splitting to release the numerous seeds, each with a plume of silky hairs

Lookalikes: Rosebay Willowherb (p.110) has flowers in long spikes and grows in drier places.

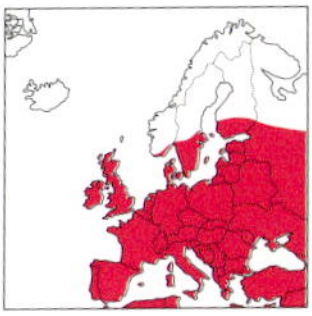

Erect, little-branched, softly hairy perennial; a conspicuous and handsome plant of marshes, streamsides, riverbanks, waysides and waste places throughout Britain and Ireland, although absent from much of Scotland. It is the largest of the willowherbs and can form thickets that more or less block small streams. The commonly used local name of Codlins-and-Cream (codlin is an old word for cooking apple) may be a whimsical reference to the colour combination of rosy petals and cream stigma and stamens.

WILLOWHERB AND EVENING PRIMROSE FAMILY, ONAGRACEAE

Broad-leaved Willowherb

Epilobium montanum

J	F	M	A	M	J
J	A	S	O	N	D

ID FACT FILE

Height: 20–80 cm

Flowers: c.1 cm across, with 4 notched, purplish-pink petals, in loose clusters; buds nod slightly

Leaves: Mostly in opposite pairs, short-stalked, narrow, oval, shallowly toothed

Fruits: Slender, downy capsules, up to 8 cm long, with many small seeds, each with a plume of silky hairs

Lookalikes: The other willowherbs differ in hairiness, flower size and other characteristics.

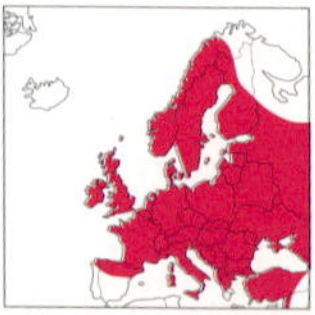

Erect, almost hairless perennial, producing clusters of leaf-rosettes from the base of the stems; a common and invasive plant of damp, shady places, woodland, waste ground and gardens, which can be very abundant on open or cultivated ground. The hairy seeds are dispersed by the wind. This is probably the commonest of our dozen or so native and introduced willowherbs, mostly plants of similar appearance and habitats; some of them are found on wet mountain rocks.

J	F	M	A	M	J
J	A	S	O	N	D

Ivy

Hedera helix

ID FACT FILE

Height: 1–5 m

Flowers: Yellowish-green, the parts in fives, in erect, stalked, domed clusters

Leaves: 5-lobed, of characteristic 'ivy' shape; those on the flowering branches elliptical, unlobed, pointed

Fruits: Spherical, flat-topped, black berries, 6–8 mm across

Lookalikes: An unmistakable plant, although the leaves vary in colour and shape.

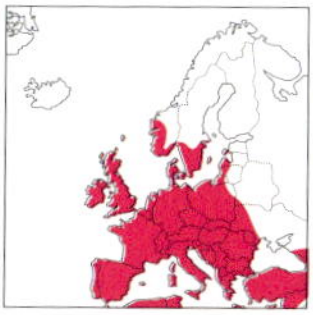

Familiar, dark green, woody climber, either trailing on the ground, climbing by means of dense, sucker-like roots or producing flowers on shrubby flowering stems. Common and widespread, Ivy is a prominent landscape feature, often carpeting the ground in woods or festooning trees, hedges and rocks, old buildings and walls. It is the last plant of the year to flower, attracting insects on sunny autumn days. Ivy is the main food plant of midsummer broods of caterpillars of the Holly Blue butterfly.

J	F	M	A	M	J
J	A	S	O	N	D

Sea Holly

Eryngium maritimum

ID FACT FILE

Height: 20–60 cm

Flowers: Blue, many, in dense, spherical heads up to 3 cm across, arranged in a cluster amongst spiny bracts

Leaves: Mostly 3-lobed, with wavy, spiny-toothed margins; margins and veins whitish; upper leaves clasping stem

Fruits: Narrowly egg-shaped; spiny

Lookalikes: A number of similar spiny plants (eryngos) are grown in gardens.

A distinctive, stiff, spiny, bluish-green, hairless perennial, forming patches; locally common on sandy seashores, sometimes on shingle. It looks superficially like the thistles (daisy and dandelion family). The plant is well adapted to its dry, harsh habitat. Deep roots enable it to reach fresh water and the waxy leaf surfaces prevent excessive water loss in the dry conditions of the beach, as well as protecting against damage from salt spray. The roots were formerly candied and sold as a sweet.

J	F	M	A	M	J
J	A	S	O	N	D

Cow Parsley or Queen Anne's Lace

Anthriscus sylvestris

ID FACT FILE

HEIGHT: 40–150 cm

FLOWERS: White, 3–4 mm across, many, in dense, flat-topped heads or umbels 3–7 cm across; a few oval bracts

LEAVES: Compound, up to 30 cm long, feathery, fern-like

FRUITS: Egg-shaped, up to 1 cm long, flattened, smooth, dark brown or black

LOOKALIKES: Hemlock (p.118) is taller and less branched, the leaves are more feathery and the stems have purple blotches.

An erect, rather robust, leafy, branched perennial; widespread and often growing in great crowds on roadsides, along hedgerows and in shadier places generally. This plant is the commonest and most familiar member of the carrot family, whitening the late spring landscape. The leaves begin to grow during winter and a few plants can be seen in flower as early as February. A variable number of plants have purplish stems and sometimes purplish leaves as well. The plant is poisonous.

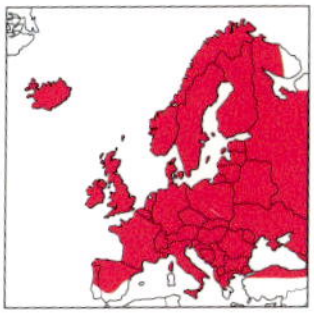

J	F	M	A	M	J
J	A	S	O	N	D

Earthnut or Pignut

Conopodium majus

ID FACT FILE

Height: 20–80 cm

Flowers: White, many, in dense, flat-topped heads or umbels, 3–7 cm across; bracts usually absent

Leaves: Feathery, with very narrow lobes, the basal ones more divided

Fruits: Egg-shaped, 3–4 mm long, with a beak

Lookalikes: The feathery leaf-segments distinguish this plant from most other members of the family; the similar leaves of Fennel (see Lookalikes of Wild Parsnip, p.119) smell of aniseed.

Slender, erect perennial, with a single stem that arises from a deeply buried, almost spherical, blackish tuber. It is a widespread plant of grassland, hedge-banks and woods, on well-drained, usually rather acid soils; it is less common in the midlands and SE of Ireland and parts of East Anglia. The tubers were long hunted as a free snack by generations of country children, although sadly this rarely happens today. Earthnuts have a western distribution in Europe; six related species occur in Spain and Portugal.

J	F	M	A	M	J
J	A	S	O	N	D

Ground Elder

Aegopodium podagraria

ID FACT FILE

HEIGHT: 30–100 cm

FLOWERS: White, many, in dense, flat-topped heads or umbels up to 6 cm across; no bracts

LEAVES: Stalked, divided 1–2 times into 3 oval or broadly spear-shaped, irregularly toothed leaflets

FRUITS: Narrowly egg-shaped, flattened, smooth, with 5 ridges

LOOKALIKES: The far-creeping habit distinguishes this familiar plant from other members of the family.

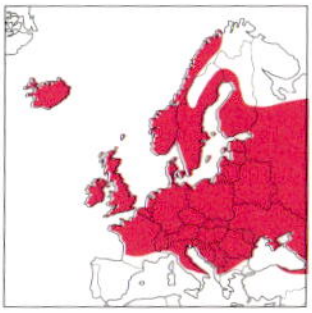

Hairless, far-creeping, rather aromatic perennial, forming large patches; common in damp, shady places, especially gardens, where it is a notorious weed. The plant spreads by means of shallowly rooted runners that are brittle and will regenerate readily to produce new plants. It is rarely found away from human habitation and is almost certainly introduced. The leaves were formerly cooked and eaten like spinach and the plant has a considerable reputation as a supposed remedy for gout.

J	F	M	A	M	J
J	A	S	O	N	D

Hemlock

Conium maculatum

ID FACT FILE

Height: 100–250 cm

Flowers: White, many, in dense, flat-topped heads or umbels 3–6 cm across; 5–6 narrowly triangular bracts

Leaves: Compound, deeply divided, fern-like

Fruits: Almost spherical, with wavy ridges, 2–3 mm long

Lookalikes: Cow Parsley (p.115) is shorter and more branched, the leaves are less feathery and the stems lack purple blotches. Hemlock Water-dropwort (*Oenanthe crocata*), of marshes and wet places, has unspotted stems and cylindrical fruits.

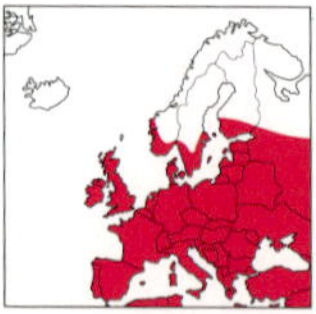

Unpleasant-smelling, hairless annual or biennial, with erect, hollow, purple-spotted stems; common by streams, on damp waste ground and road-verges, often around buildings or ruins, or on rubbish-tips. It is sometimes very abundant along new roads. A very poisonous plant indeed; its very appearance is sinister and it is not easily confused with any other species. Greek philosopher Socrates is reputed to have drunk a fatal infusion of this plant in 399 BC, as his means of execution.

J	F	M	A	M	J
J	A	S	O	N	D

Wild Parsnip

Pastinaca sativa

ID FACT FILE

Height: 30–100 cm, sometimes up to 150 cm

Flowers: Yellow, many, in dense, flat-topped heads or umbels up to 10 cm across; no bracts or sometimes 1–2 that soon fall

Leaves: Compound, with 5–11 broadly oblong, toothed leaflets

Fruits: Elliptical, flat, narrowly winged, 5–8 mm long

Lookalikes: Fennel (*Foeniculum vulgare*), with yellow flowers, has feathery leaves that smell of aniseed; it escapes from gardens on to waste ground and dry banks.

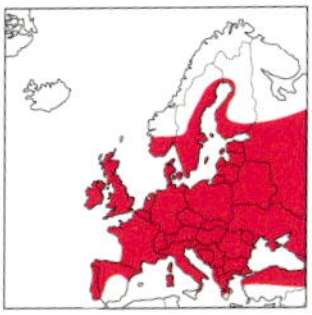

A rough-hairy, often robust, erect, aromatic biennial of dry grassland, roadsides and waste ground, usually on lime-rich soils. It occurs northwards to N Yorkshire, but is widespread only south and east of a Severn–Humber line; it is local in Ireland, where it is not native. The plant is a subspecies of garden Parsnip, a taller and more robust plant with larger seeds that sometimes escapes on to road-verges. Parsnips were a major root vegetable before potatoes were introduced from South America.

J	F	M	A	M	J
J	A	S	O	N	D

Hogweed

Heracleum sphondylium

ID FACT FILE

Height: 1–3 m

Flowers: White, or sometimes purplish-pink, many, in dense, flat-topped heads or umbels up to 25 cm across; a few, narrow bracts

Leaves: Variably compound, rough-hairy

Fruits: Oval, flat, broadly winged, 2–3 mm long

Lookalikes: Giant Hogweed (*Heracleum mantegazzianum*), introduced from the Caucasus, is a massive plant up to 5 m tall, with huge stems, leaves up to 3 m across and umbels 20–50 cm across.

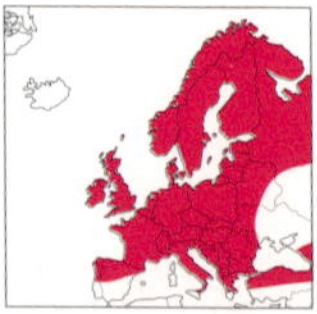

A coarse, robust, hairy, erect perennial of roadsides, hedge-banks, lush grassland, streamsides, and woodland margins and clearings. Although now disregarded as just an unsightly weed, it was a traditional food for pigs, which were once kept by most rural households. Like several other members of the carrot family, notably Giant Hogweed (see LOOKALIKES), with which it sometimes crosses, the sap causes the skin to become sensitive to sunlight, resulting in unpleasant blisters and soreness.

J	F	M	A	M	J
J	A	S	O	N	D

Wild Carrot

Daucus carota

ID FACT FILE

Height: 20–100 cm

Flowers: White or lilac, numerous, in dense, flat-topped, concave or domed heads or umbels 2–6 cm across; ruff of many deeply divided bracts

Leaves: Compound, deeply divided, fern-like

Fruits: Egg-shaped, 2–4mm long, flattened, densely spiny

Lookalikes: The ruff of deeply divided bracts gives this plant a distinctive appearance compared with other members of the family.

Annual, biennial or short-lived perennial, with a long, narrow root and erect stems; a widespread, if local, plant of dry grasslands, especially on chalk or limestone and by the sea. The concave heads of fruits are a distinctive feature of roadsides and grassland in summer. A very variable species; many plants on the coast are not more than 40 cm tall and have fleshy, shiny leaves and flat heads of fruits. Wild Carrot is a subspecies of the garden carrot, but lacks its swollen, orange root.

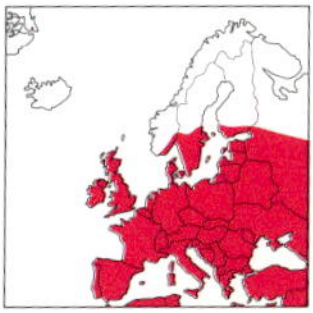

J	F	M	A	M	J
J	A	S	O	N	D

Heather or Ling

Calluna vulgaris

ID FACT FILE

Height: 20–60 cm, sometimes up to 100 cm

Flowers: Tiny, bell-shaped, pale purple, rarely lilac or white, in leafy spikes; corolla and calyx 4-lobed

Leaves: Small, overlapping in opposite rows, narrowly oblong

Fruits: Small, spherical capsules, each enclosed by dry, persistent corolla

Lookalikes: Other heathers (p.123) have larger flowers and non-overlapping leaves.

Evergreen, branched shrublet, often rather woody below; widespread and often dominant over huge areas of moors, heaths, bogs, open woods, grasslands and sand-dunes. Plants are sometimes grey-downy, especially on coastal heaths. In Scotland and elsewhere heather formerly provided thatch and bedding and was used as a source of a dye and to make a legendary beer. It is still an important source of nectar for bees. Regular burning and grazing prevents heather from becoming too overgrown.

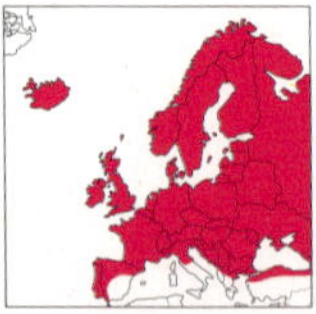

J	F	M	A	M	J
J	A	S	O	N	D

Bell Heather

Erica cinerea

ID FACT FILE

HEIGHT: 20–75 cm

FLOWERS: 4–7 mm long, sac-like, reddish-purple, rarely white, in small, elongate clusters

LEAVES: Small, very narrow, with inrolled margins, in threes

FRUITS: Small capsules, each enclosed by dry, persistent corolla

LOOKALIKES: Cross-leaved Heath (*Erica tetralix*) is greyish, downy, with leaves in fours and pink flowers; it occurs on bogs and wet heaths.

Evergreen, branched, hairless shrublet, rather woody below; widespread and often co-dominant, with Ling (p.122), over large areas of moor, dry heath, rocky ground and open wood. It provides a magnificent spectacle when in flower during late summer, especially with Dwarf Gorse (see Gorse, LOOKALIKES, p.74) on western coastal heaths. Like other heathers, it is absent from large areas of C England. The scented flowers are an important source of nectar for bees.

J	F	M	A	M	J
J	A	S	O	N	D

Bilberry, Whortleberry or Blaeberry

Vaccinium myrtillus

ID FACT FILE

Height: 20–40 cm

Flowers: Solitary or paired, 4–6 mm long, sac-like, almost spherical, pale green tinged pink

Leaves: Oval, pointed, minutely toothed, bright green, falling in autumn

Fruits: Spherical, bluish-black berries 5–8 mm across

Lookalikes: Related species of more local distribution, with black or red berries, are found on bogs, moors and mountains.

Little-branched, hairless shrublet of moors, heaths and open woods of birch, oak and pine on well-drained acid soils; often very abundant, but scarce in C England and E Anglia and much of the midlands of Ireland. The edible, sweet berries were formerly gathered commercially by country people, but are now encountered only rarely in shops and restaurants in Britain and Ireland. They are still extensively collected in C and E Europe, and are excellent eaten raw or cooked in tarts, jelly or jam. They also make a purplish dye.

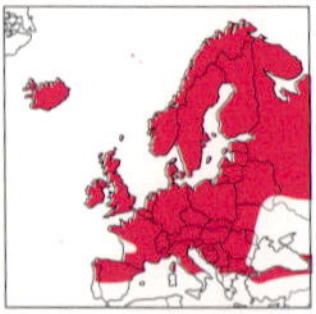

J	F	M	A	M	J
J	A	S	O	N	D

Cowslip

Primula veris

ID FACT FILE

Height: 10–35 cm

Flowers: 8–15 mm across, golden yellow, with orange spot at the base of each petal-lobe, in nodding 1-sided cluster; calyx bell-shaped, pleated, pale green

Leaves: All in a basal rosette, more or less oval, abruptly contracted into stalk, indistinctly toothed, wrinkled

Fruits: Capsules enclosed within persistent calyx-tube

Lookalikes: Hybrids with Primrose have larger flowers.

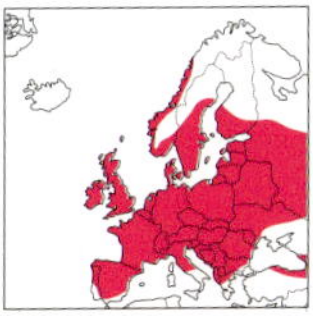

Tufted, downy perennial of old meadows and pastures, railway cuttings and embankments, coastal cliffs and road-verges, usually on lime-rich or clay soils. One of the most familiar and best-loved of all our native wild flowers, although it is local in Scotland. Regrettably reduced in numbers by the destruction of its grassland habitat by modern agriculture, it is now returning on motorway verges and other newly sown grassland. It sometimes crosses with Primrose (p.126) to form a handsome, polyanthus-like hybrid, False Oxlip.

J	F	M	A	M	J
J	A	S	O	N	D

Sometimes from November in mild districts.

Primrose

Primula vulgaris

ID FACT FILE

Height: 10–25 cm

Flowers: 20–40 mm across, solitary, pale yellow with darker centre, richly scented; calyx bell-shaped, pleated, green

Leaves: In a basal rosette, more or less oblong, tapered into stalk, indistinctly toothed, wrinkled, downy beneath

Fruits: Almost spherical capsules enclosed within persistent calyx-tube

Lookalikes: Hybrids with Cowslip (p.125) have flowers grouped in a head.

Tufted perennial of woodland, scrub, grassy banks, railway embankments, sea-cliffs and mountain ledges. In some areas it has been exterminated by digging up and removal to gardens. It sometimes crosses with Cowslip and occasional pink-flowered plants probably represent crosses with garden primroses and polyanthus. Long loved as the *Prima Rosa* (Latin: first rose) of spring, it was also a favourite flower of Victorian politician Benjamin Disraeli, whose 19 April birthday is Primrose Day.

J	F	M	A	M	J
J	A	S	O	N	D

Yellow Pimpernel

Lysimachia nemorum

ID FACT FILE

Height: 10–45 cm

Flowers: In pairs, arising from leaf-axils, dish-shaped, yellow, 6–9 mm across, on very slender stalks

Leaves: In opposite pairs, heart-shaped, pointed

Fruits: Spherical capsules, enclosed within – and much shorter than – the persistent calyx; splitting by 5 teeth when ripe

Lookalikes: Creeping Jenny (p.128) has bell-shaped, larger flowers on shorter, thicker stalks.

Delicate, creeping perennial of woodland rides and damp, shady places, especially on more acid soils. It is generally widespread throughout Britain and Ireland, but often overlooked, despite a long flowering season. Thc perennial, evergreen habit readily distinguishes it from Scarlet Pimpernel (p.130), which can have flowers of various colours (but never yellow). The first half of the scientific name commemorates Lysimachos, from Thrace, one of Alexander the Great's generals.

J	F	M	A	M	J
J	A	S	O	N	D

Creeping Jenny

Lysimachia nummularia

ID FACT FILE

Height: 10–45 cm

Flowers: In pairs arising from leaf-axils, bell-shaped, yellow, 1–2 cm across, on short stalks

Leaves: In opposite pairs, oval, blunt

Fruits: Capsules not observed in Britain

Lookalikes: Yellow Pimpernel (p.127) has dish-shaped, much smaller flowers on very slender stalks.

Elegant, far-creeping perennial of lake-shores, ditches, path-sides and damp, usually shady, grassy places; often overlooked. This plant is most commonly to be observed, often as a weed, in cottage gardens and around villages. It is rare in Scotland and much of Ireland, especially the south; it is introduced in Cornwall. The creeping stems root at each leaf pair – the plant does not set seed in Britain and Ireland, but reproduces readily from rooting vegetative fragments.

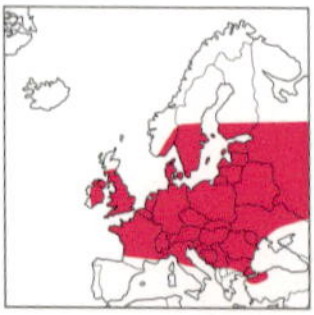

J	F	M	A	M	J
J	A	S	O	N	D

Yellow Loosestrife

Lysimachia vulgaris

ID FACT FILE

Height: 40–160 cm

Flowers: Cup-shaped, 15–18 mm across, with 5 petals and 5 sepals, clustered in loose, branched heads

Leaves: In opposite pairs or in threes or fours, short-stalked, oval to spear-shaped, with black dots

Fruits: Spherical capsules

Lookalikes: Dotted Loosestrife (*Lysimachia punctata*) is a garden escape with flowers 2–3 cm across in long, dense clusters.

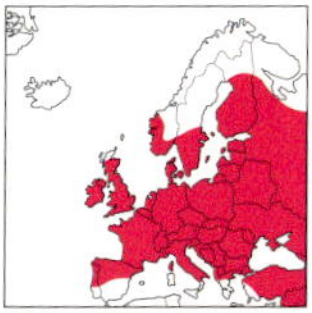

An erect perennial, spreading by rhizomes and forming clumps in marshes, wet woods, shores of lakes and gravel-pits, riverbanks and near houses as an escape from gardens. It is widespread, if rather local, throughout Britain and Ireland, except for much of N and E Scotland. This plant is not related to Purple Loosestrife (p.107), although they occur in similar marshland and wet habitats. 'Loosestrife' may refer to a calming effect that these plants supposedly have on livestock.

J	F	M	A	M	J
J	A	S	O	N	D

Scarlet Pimpernel

Anagallis arvensis

ID FACT FILE

Height: 5–50 cm

Flowers: In pairs, arising from leaf-axils, dish-shaped, 4–8 mm across, scarlet, with a purple centre, sometimes flesh-coloured (rarely blue or lilac)

Leaves: In opposite pairs, short-stalked, oval to spear-shaped, sometimes slightly fleshy

Fruits: Spherical capsules c.5 mm across, splitting round the middle

Lookalikes: Yellow Pimpernel (p.127) is perennial, with slightly larger, yellow flowers, and grows in damp, shady places.

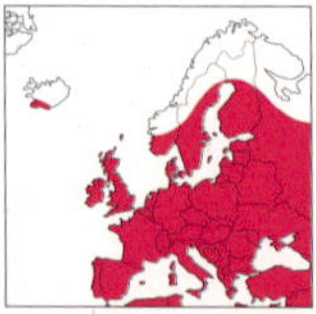

A prostrate, hairless, ascending or weakly erect annual or biennial, with square stems. It is a common plant of cultivated land, waysides, sand-dunes and open, damp or sandy places near the sea, and the prettiest of our common weeds. The flowers open only in bright sunshine – hence its other name, 'Poor Man's Weatherglass' – although they close in late afternoon as well. Plants with flesh-coloured flowers are locally common on the coasts of Ireland, SW England and elsewhere.

J	F	M	A	M	J
J	A	S	O	N	D

Thrift or Sea Pink

Armeria maritima

ID FACT FILE

HEIGHT: 5–15 cm, sometimes up to 35 cm

FLOWERS: 5–10 mm across, funnel-shaped, scented, pink, in dense, rounded heads 1–3 cm across, with papery scales surrounding the base; papery, persistent calyx

LEAVES: All basal, grass-like, pointed, slightly fleshy

FRUITS: Small, 1-seeded, dry, papery

LOOKALIKES: A distinctive plant of the seaside that is hard to confuse with any other.

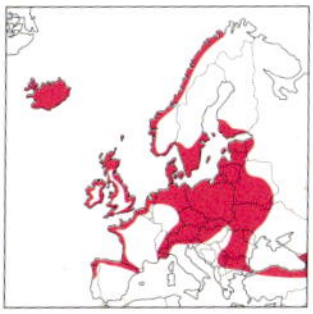

Low-growing perennial, with tufts of leaves arising from woody stems, forming extensive patches and mats. One of the commonest and most characteristic plants of cliffs, coastal rocks and saltmarshes, also on mountain rocks and grasslands, mine spoil-heaps and sometimes on lake-shores, as at Killarney in Co. Kerry. A very variable species; inland in Lincolnshire, a tall, erect subspecies grows in a few surviving fragments of heathland. Compact, darker-flowered plants are widely grown in gardens.

J	F	M	A	M	J
J	A	S	O	N	D

Common Sea-lavender

Limonium vulgare

ID FACT FILE

HEIGHT: 20–40 cm, sometimes up to 70 cm

FLOWERS: 5–6 mm across, funnel-shaped, bluish-lilac, in a dense, 1-sided, flat-topped, branched cluster

LEAVES: All basal, stalked, spear-shaped or elliptical, more or less pointed, fleshy

FRUITS: Small, 1-seeded, dry, papery

LOOKALIKES: Lax-flowered Sea-lavender (*Limonium humile*), with stems up to 40 cm tall, branched in upper half, and flowers in longer, looser spikes, has a similar distribution but also occurs in Ireland.

Erect, hairless perennial, with rather woody, branched rhizomes and leafless stems, a conspicuous feature of muddy saltmarshes and sometimes coastal cliffs, rocks and shingle beaches. It is widespread and often common on coasts north to the Firth of Forth, although absent from Ireland (but see Lax-flowered Sea-lavender, LOOKALIKES). In July and August, it tints saltmarshes with its distinctive, lavender-like colour. The dried flowers are sometimes used in flower-arranging.

J	F	M	A	M	J
J	A	S	O	N	D

Centaury

Centaurium erythraea

ID FACT FILE

Height: 10–30 cm, sometimes up to 50 cm

Flowers: Pink, funnel-shaped, 5–8 mm across in a dense, branched, more or less flat-topped cluster

Leaves: Basal leaves oval, stem leaves much smaller and narrower

Fruits: Small, cylindrical capsules

Lookalikes: There are a number of other, rarer, pink-flowered species of centaury, all of them strictly coastal.

Erect, hairless biennial or short-lived perennial, usually with a single stem, of dry grassland, sea-cliffs and sand-dunes. This attractive wild flower is our commonest native gentian relative; it is generally widespread, but it is local and mostly coastal in Scotland. It is a variable species, especially where it grows on the coast – here, dwarf and narrow-leaved variants occur. The plant has healing properties and an infusion made from it has long been used as a tonic to aid digestion.

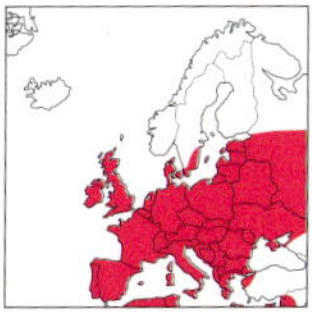

J	F	M	A	M	J
J	A	S	O	N	D

Yellow-wort

Blackstonia perfoliata

ID FACT FILE

Height: 10–60 cm

Flowers: Yellow, 8–15 mm across, bowl-shaped, in a loose, more or less flat-topped cluster

Leaves: Basal leaves oval, the stem-leaves in opposite fused pairs, almost triangular

Fruits: Small, cylindrical capsules

Lookalikes: The combination of yellow flowers and fused pairs of bluish-grey leaves is unmistakable.

Erect, hairless, pale bluish-green annual of dry grassland, fens and sand-dunes, especially on lime-rich soils. It is widespread but local, northwards to Yorkshire and Co. Sligo, although is now expanding its range in N England, where it has spread via commercial wild flower seed-mixtures. This plant has been used as a tonic to aid digestion and as the source of a yellow dye. The first half of the scientific name commemorates the English apothecary and botanist John Blackstone (1712–53).

J	F	M	A	M	J
J	A	S	O	N	D

Autumn Felwort

Gentianella amarella

ID FACT FILE

Height: 5–30 cm

Flowers: 12–20 mm long, bell-shaped, dull purple or pinkish-purple, with 4–5 spreading lobes, fringed around the mouth

Leaves: In opposite pairs, broadly spear-shaped, tinged purple

Fruits: Small cylindrical capsules

Lookalikes: Spring Gentian (*Gentiana verna*), a perennial with larger, deep blue flowers, occurs in limestone grassland in the Galway Bay region of Ireland and in Upper Teesdale, Yorkshire.

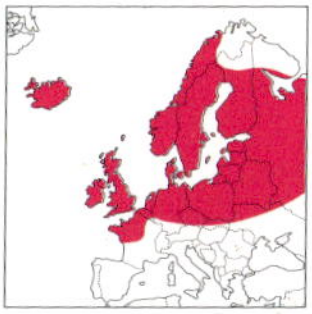

Erect, hairless annual or biennial of grassland on chalk and limestone, sea-cliffs and sand-dunes. This plant sometimes appears in quantity in chalk grassland during late summer, when few other plants are starting to flower. It is rather local, especially in Scotland and Ireland. Felworts are very similar to the true gentians of the Alps and elsewhere, but differ in small features of the flowers, especially the fringes of hairs at the mouth of the corolla, which are absent in gentians.

J	F	M	A	M	J
J	A	S	O	N	D

Bogbean or Buckbean

Menyanthes trifoliata

ID FACT FILE

Height: 10–35 cm

Flowers: Pink or white, c.15 mm across, bell-shaped, with 5 spreading, hairy petal-lobes, up to 12 in a long cluster

Leaves: Long-stalked, the stalk with a broad, sheathing base and bearing 3 stalked, elliptical leaflets

Fruits: Small, almost spherical capsule

Lookalikes: Water Violet (*Hottonia palustris*), a local plant of ponds in E England, has feathery leaves and hairless petal-lobes.

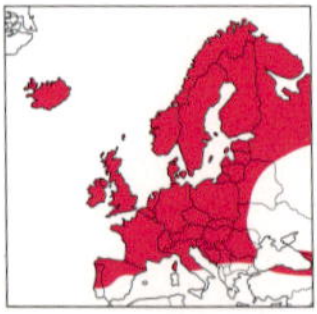

Handsome, hairless, aquatic perennial, far-creeping with stout, creeping rhizome; sometimes abundant in shallow lakes, ponds, moorland lochans or tarns and bog-pools. Common in much of N and W Britain, and in Ireland, this plant has disappeared from many parts of S England. The leaves are bitter to the taste and have been used to flavour beer. A good stand of the plant in open water during May and June provides one of the finest floral displays in Britain or Ireland.

J	F	M	A	M	J
J	A	S	O	N	D

Field Madder

Sherardia arvensis

ID FACT FILE

HEIGHT: 10–40 cm

FLOWERS: Lilac, funnel-shaped with 4 spreading petal-lobes, 2–3 mm across, in a dense cluster surrounded by 8–10 bracts

LEAVES: Narrow, stiff, spear-shaped, pointed, in whorls of 4–6

FRUITS: 2-lobed, bristly, crowned by persistent, enlarged calyx-teeth

LOOKALIKES: Squinancywort (*Asperula cynanchica*) is a larger, perennial plant, with 2–4 leaves in a whorl, and without bracts around the flowers.

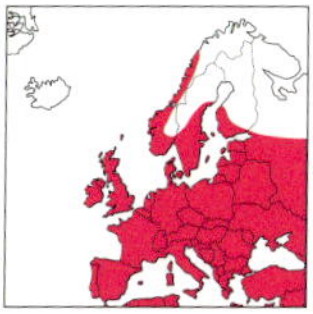

Prostrate or sprawling annual, with 4-angled stems covered with minute, down-curved prickles; a widespread, attractive plant of dry grasslands, grassy walls and banks, unmanicured lawns and arable fields, especially on lime-rich soils. It is widespread over much of Britain, although rare in N Scotland, and rather local over much of Ireland. The first half of the scientific name commemorates William Sherard (1659–1728), a notable professor of botany at Oxford.

J	F	M	A	M	J
J	A	S	O	N	D

Sweet Woodruff

Galium odoratum

ID FACT FILE

Height: 10–25 cm

Flowers: Creamy white, 4–7 mm across, funnel-shaped, with 4–5 spreading petal-lobes, in loose, long-stalked, domed clusters

Leaves: Spear-shaped, shiny, up to 5 cm long, in whorls of 6–9

Fruits: Tiny, 2-lobed, covered with hooked hairs

Lookalikes: Other white members of the bedstraw and madder family have branched stems and more elongate or branched flower-clusters.

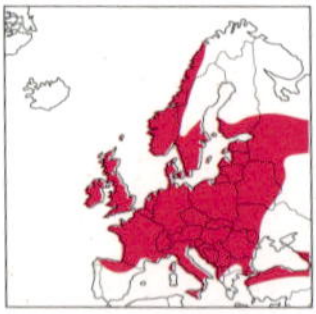

Almost hairless perennial, with creeping underground stems and erect, unbranched, 4-angled leafy stems; widespread in woods and shady places on lime-rich soils, especially where the ground is slightly damp and there is leaf-mould. The plant smells of new-mown hay when dried and was formerly popular for stuffing mattresses, strewing on floors and scenting linen. It is a mild digestive tonic and has been used to flavour drinks; it remains a popular plant for the cottage garden.

J	F	M	A	M	J
J	A	S	O	N	D

Lady's Bedstraw

Galium verum

ID FACT FILE

Height: 10–120 cm

Flowers: Yellow, scented, 2–3.5 mm across, with 4 spreading petal-lobes, in long, dense, often branched clusters

Leaves: Very narrow, 1-veined, sharp-pointed, in whorls of 8–12

Fruits: 2-lobed, smooth, 1–1.5 mm long

Lookalikes: Squinancywort (*Asperula cynanchica*) is a larger perennial plant, with 2–4 leaves in a whorl, and pink or white flowers. Hedge Bedstraw (p.140) has white flowers.

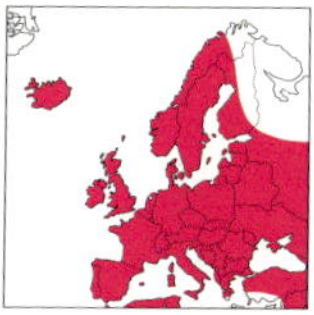

Attractive, finely hairy, erect or sprawling perennial, with creeping, underground stems, a widespread plant of dry grasslands, hedgebanks, sand-dunes, shingle beaches, sometimes in churchyards and on lawns, especially on lime-rich soils. Hay made from this useful plant was popular for stuffing mattresses, not only for its sweet scent but also because it deters fleas and other vermin. Lady's Bedstraw was formerly used as a substitute for rennet to curdle cheese. The underground stems yield a red dye.

J	F	M	A	M	J
J	A	S	O	N	D

Hedge Bedstraw

Galium mollugo

ID FACT FILE

HEIGHT: 30–160 cm

FLOWERS: White, 2–3 mm across, with 4 spreading petal-lobes, in a loose, much-branched cluster

LEAVES: Narrow, oblong, pointed, with rough-prickly margins, in whorls of 6–8

FRUITS: 2-lobed, rough, purplish or greyish, 1–2 mm long

LOOKALIKES: Heath Bedstraw (*Galium saxatile*), a plant of heaths and pastures on poor soils, is not more than 35 cm tall, with mostly prostrate stems and leaves in whorls of 4–6.

Erect or spreading perennial, with long, underground runners and often hairy, but not prickly, stems; a widespread plant of dry grassland, woodland clearings and hedges. The perennial bedstraws, plants of grasslands and marshes, and all except Lady's Bedstraw (p.139) with white flowers, are a difficult group of plants to distinguish from one another. Occasional hybrids with Lady's Bedstraw, which occur where the two grow together and cross, have pale yellow flowers.

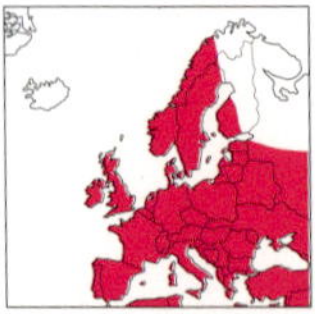

J	F	M	A	M	J
J	A	S	O	N	D

Goosegrass or Cleavers

Galium aparine

ID FACT FILE

Height: 50–180 cm

Flowers: Greenish-white or white, 1.5–2 mm across, with 4 spreading petal-lobes, in a loose, few-flowered cluster

Leaves: Narrow, oblong, pointed, prickly with hooked bristles, in whorls of 6–9

Fruits: 2-lobed, densely covered with hooked bristles, 3–6 mm long

Lookalikes: Hedge Bedstraw (p.140) is perennial with smooth rather than bristly stems and dense clusters of white flowers.

A scrambling or climbing, bristly annual, with 4-angled stems, of scrub, woodland margins, hedge-banks, cultivated land and shingle beaches. The bristly fruits cling readily to clothes and animal fur – one rarely returns from a country walk without a few in one's socks or the dog's coat – effectively dispersing the seeds. Indeed, the whole plant will stick to clothes like 'velcro', demonstrating how the bristles are its means of support. A variable species: plants from cultivated ground often have smaller fruits.

J	F	M	A	M	J
J	A	S	O	N	D

Field Bindweed

Convolvulus arvensis

ID FACT FILE

Height: 50–200 cm

Flowers: White, or pink variously striped with white, funnel-shaped, 15–35 mm across, slightly scented, 1–3 on stalks about as long as the leaves

Leaves: Oblong, triangular, spear- or arrow-shaped

Fruits: Almost spherical, 2-celled capsules

Lookalikes: Hedge Bindweed (p.143) is a larger plant with usually white flowers 3–6 cm across.

Slender, elegant, often hairy perennial, arising from an extensive, branched root system, with numerous twining (anti-clockwise) stems, which exude a white milky juice when cut. This is a familiar and abundant plant of cultivated and waste ground, also amongst grass, either prostrate or climbing other plants and wire-netting fences. Even quite small fragments of the deep roots can grow into new plants. The flowers close during dull or wet weather and in late afternoon. A very variable species.

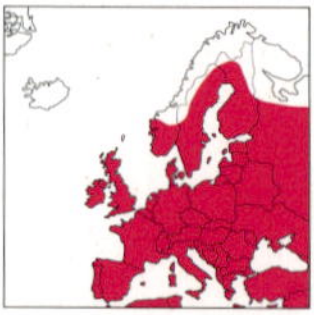

J	F	M	A	M	J
J	A	S	O	N	D

Hedge Bindweed

Calystegia sepium

ID FACT FILE

Height: 1–3 m

Flowers: White, sometimes pink or pink and white, funnel-shaped, 3–6 cm across, unscented; 2 bracts, sometimes inflated, at base

Leaves: Heart- or arrow-shaped

Fruits: Spherical, 1-celled capsules, enclosed by persistent sepals

Lookalikes: Field Bindweed (p.142) is a smaller plant with white or pink flowers 15–35 mm across; Sea Bindweed (*Calystegia soldanella*), with short stems, round leaves and pink flowers, occurs on sand-dunes.

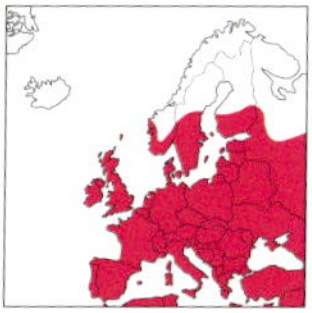

A perennial climber, with tough, twining stems, that exude a white, milky juice when cut; a frequent plant of wood margins, scrub, marshes and waste ground, too often a serious garden weed. Sometimes hedges, banks, wire-netting fences and the wires supporting telegraph poles are festooned with a dense growth of this plant. A variable species; an introduced subspecies has more vigorous leafy growth and larger flowers 6–8 cm across, with strongly inflated bracts at the base.

J	F	M	A	M	J
J	A	S	O	N	D

Viper's Bugloss

Echium vulgare

ID FACT FILE

Height: 30–100 cm

Flowers: Blue, with purplish-red buds, tubular, 1–2 cm long, in curved, 1-sided clusters forming a tall spike; 4–5 stamens, the longer ones protruding

Leaves: Elliptical or strap-shaped, the upper ones narrower

Fruits: 4 nutlets

Lookalikes: Borage (*Borago officinalis*) has oval or spear-shaped leaves and flowers with 5 widely spreading segments, in loose clusters; it is a garden escape.

Bristly, erect annual or biennial of dry grassland, waysides, roadside rubble, bare chalk or gravel, and shingle beaches. Widespread but local in England, it is rarer in Scotland and occurs in Ireland mainly near the E coast. The flowers are very striking, with their purplish-red buds; in quantity they can be a wonderful show of blue, not a common colour amongst our native wild flowers. This plant causes no trouble in Britain, but is a major weed in parts of the USA where it has been introduced.

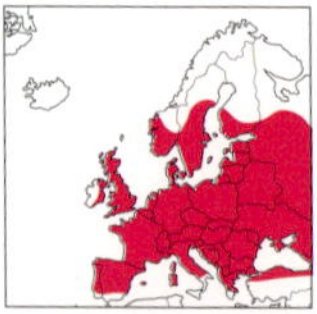

J	F	M	A	M	J
J	A	S	O	N	D

Comfrey

Symphytum officinale

ID FACT FILE

Height: 50–120 cm

Flowers: White or violet-purple, pinkish or blue, tubular, 12–18 mm long, in 1-sided clusters

Leaves: Broadly spear-shaped, pointed, the upper ones stalkless

Fruits: 4 smooth, black, shiny nutlets

Lookalikes: The most widespread of several comfreys, mostly garden escapes. Tuberous Comfrey (*Symphytum tuberosum*), up to 40 cm tall with pale yellow flowers, is common in woods in N Britain.

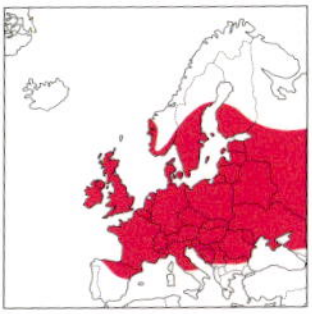

Robust, erect, branched, rough-hairy perennial, with winged stems, forming large, untidy patches in hedgerows, waysides, ditches, damp grassland and the banks of streams and rivers. This is a most vigorous and valuable plant; in recent years it and related species have assumed almost a cult status amongst herbal healers and gardeners. Comfrey reduces inflammation and aids healing; the leaves can be eaten like spinach or fried in batter; and the whole plant makes a mineral-rich garden compost.

COMFREY AND FORGET-ME-NOT FAMILY, BORAGINACEAE

J	F	M	A	M	J
J	A	S	O	N	D

Hound's-tongue

Cynoglossum officinale

ID FACT FILE

Height: 30–60 cm

Flowers: Reddish-purple, 5–6 mm across, in 1-sided clusters

Leaves: Oblong or spear-shaped, with dense, grey-silky hairs

Fruits: 4 egg-shaped, flattened nutlets, covered with short, hooked spines

Lookalikes: Borage (*Borago officinalis*) has larger, blue flowers in looser, spreading clusters; it is a garden escape.

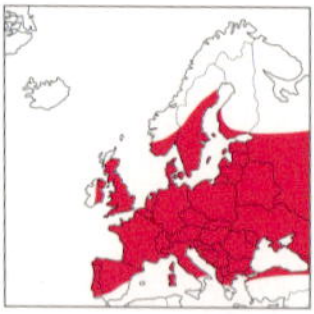

A softly hairy, erect, leafy biennial, with winged stems; widespread but local in dry, open, stony and grassy places and sand-dunes, especially on chalk and sand. It is widespread in England and Wales but rare in Scotland and Ireland. The plant smells strongly of mice when bruised (the chemical released is acetamide) and is unpalatable to grazing animals; for this reason it sometimes occurs in abundance around rabbit burrows. The spiny fruits adhere readily to clothing and animal fur, thus dispersing the seeds.

J	F	M	A	M	J
J	A	S	O	N	D

Field Forget-me-not

Myosotis arvensis

ID FACT FILE

Height: 5–25 cm

Flowers: Pale blue, with a yellow eye, saucer-shaped, 3–5 mm across, in leafless, 1-sided, rather flat-topped clusters

Leaves: Elliptical, the upper ones smaller, spear-shaped

Fruits: 4 nutlets, enclosed within calyx

Lookalikes: Two other forget-me-nots of dry, open ground have flowers 2–3 mm across: Early Forget-me-not (*Myosotis ramosissima*) has blue flowers; Changing Forget-me-not (*Mysosotis discolor*) has flowers that open yellow and change to blue.

Erect annual of open and disturbed ground, especially arable fields. The flowers of the forget-me-nots demonstrate well the characteristic structure found in the comfrey and forget-me-not family. The clusters are short and condensed in bud, but the main stalk lengthens and curves as the flowers open to produce a shape reminiscent of the curled tail of the scorpion. From this derives an older name for Forget-me-not, Scorpion-grass, which comes to us from both French and German.

J	F	M	A	M	J
J	A	S	O	N	D

Water Forget-me-not

Myosotis scorpioides

ID FACT FILE

Height: 10–40 cm

Flowers: Saucer-shaped, pale blue, with a yellow eye, rarely pink or white, 8–10 mm across, in leafless, 1-sided, flat-topped clusters; 5 triangular calyx-teeth

Leaves: In opposite pairs, spear- or spoon-shaped, blunt, the upper ones smaller

Fruits: 4 black, shiny nutlets, enclosed in the calyx

Lookalikes: The short, triangular calyx-teeth distinguish this plant from other species of forget-me-not of wet places.

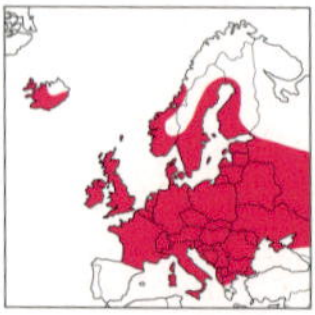

Erect, hairless to slightly hairy, pale green perennial with creeping stolons or runners; widespread and often abundant beside and in streams, in marshes and wet woods, especially rides and glades, and damp meadows. This plant can be a fine sight when in flower. Other similar forget-me-nots occur in wet places: for example, Creeping Forget-me-not (*Myosotis secunda*), of acid marshes and bogs, especially in N and W Britain and Ireland, which is hairier and has flowers 6–8 mm across.

J	F	M	A	M	J
J	A	S	O	N	D

Bugle

Ajuga reptans

Erect perennial with long runners, the stems hairy on opposite sides at each leaf pair; widespread and often common in woods, especially rides and glades, hedges and damp meadows. The upper stems and leaves have something of the blue tint of the flowers. The plant has had a wide range of herbal uses, notably to staunch bleeding. Long established as a cottage garden plant, it remains popular as a cover plant for rockeries and borders, especially variants with bronze or multicoloured leaves.

ID FACT FILE

Height: 10–40 cm

Flowers: Blue, rarely pink or white, 14–18 mm, in clusters amongst leafy bracts, tubular, 1–2 cm long, in a tall spike

Leaves: In opposite pairs, oval, stalked, obscurely toothed, the upper ones smaller

Fruits: 4 nutlets

Lookalikes: The blue flowers in tall spikes distinguish Bugle from other members of the mint family; Skullcap (p.151) has flowers in pairs in a loose, 1-sided spike.

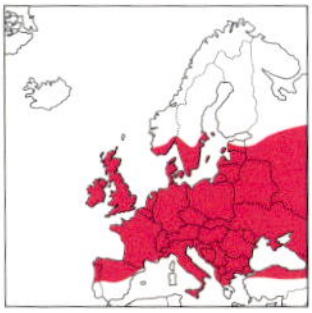

J	F	M	A	M	J
J	A	S	O	N	D

Wood Sage

Teucrium scorodonia

ID FACT FILE

Height: 20–50 cm

Flowers: Greenish-yellow, sometimes white or marked with red, 8–10 mm long, in pairs grouped in loose, spike-like clusters; hairy calyx

Leaves: In opposite pairs, triangular to oval, with heart-shaped base

Fruits: 4 nutlets

Lookalikes: Yellow Archangel (p.155) has a creeping rather than shrubby habit and has larger flowers in late spring.

Erect, branched, rather dowdy shrublet of heaths, scrub, dry, sandy or limestone banks, and rocky ground. It grows on both lime-rich and acid soils; research has shown that the adaptation of plants to grow on either soil type has a genetically controlled basis. The flowers appear dull, but they are neatly structured and sometimes attractively and richly marked with red. The plant was formerly used to flavour and preserve beer and has been used as a medicinal herb with healing properties.

J	F	M	A	M	J
J	A	S	O	N	D

Skullcap

Scutellaria galericulata

ID FACT FILE

Height: 10–50 cm

Flowers: Blue, with whitish-spotted lip, 1–2 cm long, in pairs in a loose, 1-sided spike

Leaves: In opposite pairs, ovate or broadly spear-shaped, with a few round teeth

Fruits: 4 nutlets

Lookalikes: Bugle (p.149) has more numerous blue flowers clustered in a denser spike.

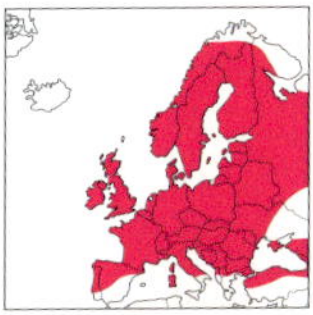

Erect, downy perennial, with creeping, rooting runners, of marshes, banks and margins of streams and rivers, damp woods and meadows. It is a widespread and sometimes common plant, but is local in E Scotland and in Ireland. Lesser Skullcap (*Scutellaria minor*), a smaller plant up to 15 cm tall, with more or less toothless leaves and purple-spotted, lilac flowers, is found on damp heaths and moors, mostly in the west. It sometimes crosses with Skullcap to form hybrids.

J	F	M	A	M	J
J	A	S	O	N	D

Hemp-nettle

Galeopsis tetrahit

ID FACT FILE

Height: 10–50 cm

Flowers: Pink or whitish, sometimes pale yellow, with darker markings, 15–20 mm long, in dense whorls; bristly calyx

Leaves: In opposite pairs, oval or broadly spear-shaped, pointed, coarsely toothed

Fruits: 4 nutlets

Lookalikes: Red Dead-nettle (p.154) is a smaller plant with pinkish-purple flowers and pointed but not bristly calyx-teeth.

Coarsely hairy annual, the square stems with hairs on opposite sides; a widespread but rather local plant of open woodland, heaths, marshes and cultivated land. It is much less common as an arable weed than formerly. This plant is famous amongst plant evolutionists as the first species to be recreated in the botanic garden by crossing, followed by doubling up of the genetic material of the hybrid, of the two related species from which it was thought to have been derived in the wild. There are five similar species of hemp-nettle, mostly uncommon.

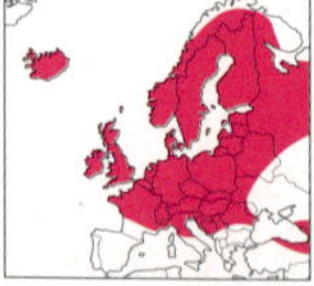

J	F	M	A	M	J
J	A	S	O	N	D

White Dead-nettle

Lamium album

ID FACT FILE

Height: 20–80 cm

Flowers: Creamy white, 18–25 mm long, in conspicuous, compact whorls; upper lip of corolla domed; bristle-like calyx-teeth

Leaves: In opposite pairs, triangular to oval, pointed, coarsely toothed

Fruits: 4 nutlets

Lookalikes: Yellow Archangel (p.155) has yellow flowers.

Hairy, erect perennial of roadsides, hedges, shady waste ground and gardens. It occurs throughout Britain but is rare or local in N and W Scotland and in W and SW Ireland, where it is probably introduced. It rarely occurs very far from buildings, roads or paths. One of the plant's local names is Adam-and-Eve-in-the-Bower, alluding to the pair of black and yellow stamens that lie side by side in the domed upper lip of the flower. The flowers are attractive to bumblebees. Dead-nettles lack stinging hairs and are not related to Stinging Nettle (p.12).

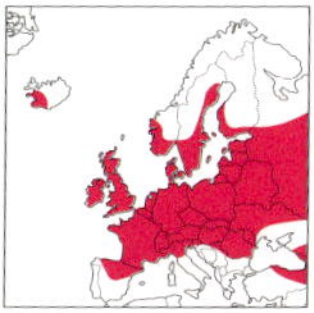

J	F	M	A	M	J
J	A	S	O	N	D

All through mild winters.

Red Dead-nettle

Lamium purpureum

ID FACT FILE

Height: 10–40 cm

Flowers: Pinkish-purple, rarely pale pink or white, 10–18 mm long, in conspicuous whorls; calyx-teeth pointed, not bristly

Leaves: In opposite pairs, oval, heart-shaped at the base, pointed, toothed

Fruits: 4 nutlets

Lookalikes: Hemp-nettle (p.152) is a larger, coarser plant with pink flowers and bristle-like calyx-teeth.

Downy, ascending or spreading annual, aromatic when crushed, the whole plant often purple-tinged; ubiquitous on cultivated and waste ground and a familiar garden weed. The flowers are very attractive to bumblebees. Red Dead-nettle is one of the first flowers to appear in late winter and early spring, along with Chickweed (p.25), Shepherd's Purse (p.47) and Groundsel (p.215). Dead-nettles do not have stinging hairs and are not at all related to Stinging Nettle (p.12).

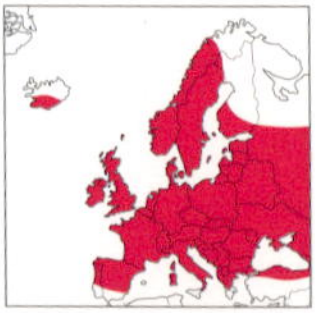

J	F	M	A	M	J
J	A	S	O	N	D

Yellow Archangel

Lamiastrum galeobdolon

ID FACT FILE

Height: 20–50 cm

Flowers: Yellow, marked with reddish-brown, 15–25 mm long, 6–10 in conspicuous whorls; hairy stamens

Leaves: In opposite pairs, oval to spear-shaped, stalked, pointed, toothed

Fruits: 4 nutlets

Lookalikes: The hairy stamens distinguish this plant from the dead-nettles. White Dead-nettle (p.153) has white flowers.

Distinctive, erect perennial, with leafy runners, often forming quite extensive patches, growing in woods, coppices and shady hedges. It is widespread in England and Wales, but very rare in Scotland and occurs in just a few places near the east coast of Ireland. It tends to grow on more lime-rich soils. A vigorous garden variant with white-spotted leaves and far-creeping runners escapes and is locally common on shady banks and lanesides. The origin of the attractive English name is obscure.

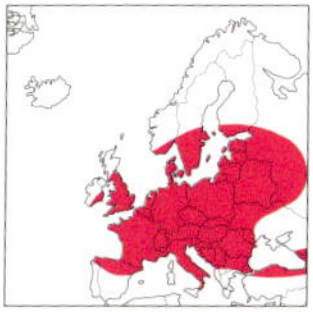

J	F	M	A	M	J
J	A	S	O	N	D

Black Horehound

Ballota nigra

ID FACT FILE

Height: 30–80 cm

Flowers: Dull purple, 12–18 mm long, in dense but well-spaced whorls up the stem; funnel-shaped calyx

Leaves: In opposite pairs, oval or heart-shaped, stalked, coarsely toothed

Fruits: 4 nutlets

Lookalikes: Basil Thyme (*Clinopodium vulgare*) has little smell, and fewer, slightly larger, bright purplish-pink flowers; it grows mostly in grassland or hedge-banks on lime-rich soils.

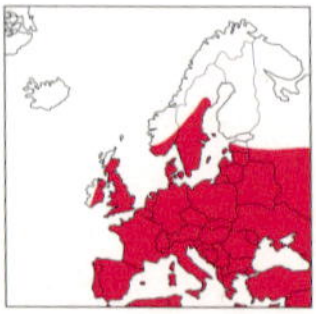

Rather scruffy, erect, hairy perennial, with leafy stems, the whole plant giving off a strong, unpleasant smell when bruised. It occurs on waste and disturbed ground, along hedges and by paths and roadsides, sometimes in quite shady places. It is widespread in England and Wales, but absent from much of Scotland and very local in Ireland, where it is introduced. White Horehound (*Marrubium vulgare*), with white-woolly leaves and inconspicuous whitish flowers, is much less common.

J	F	M	A	M	J
J	A	S	O	N	D

Betony

Stachys officinalis

ID FACT FILE

Height: 10–100 cm

Flowers: Rich reddish-purple, rarely pink or white, 12–18 mm long, many, in a dense, cylindrical spike

Leaves: In opposite pairs, mostly basal, oblong or narrowly oval, with heart-shaped base, stalked, coarsely toothed

Fruits: 4 nutlets

Lookalikes: Marsh Woundwort (p.158) has unstalked leaves; Hedge Woundwort (p.159) has a strong smell when bruised. Both are more robust with leafier stems.

Erect, unbranched, variably hairy perennial, of open woods, scrub, heaths, dry grassland and coastal cliffs. It is widespread, if rather local, in England but scattered and rare in Scotland and Ireland. Plants from the most exposed coastal cliffs in SW England and elsewhere are often dwarfed. Small plants of this type, also those with pink flowers, are sometimes grown in gardens. Betony has long been used medicinally for its reputed range of healing and sedative properties.

J	F	M	A	M	J
J	A	S	O	N	D

Marsh Woundwort

Stachys palustris

ID FACT FILE

Height: 20–120 cm

Flowers: Pinkish-purple, 12–15 mm long, in whorls, forming a dense, pyramidal spike

Leaves: In opposite pairs, spear-shaped, short-stalked or stalkless, coarsely toothed

Fruits: 4 nutlets

Lookalikes: Hedge Woundwort (p.159) has a stronger smell when bruised, solid stems, stalked leaves and darker red flowers.

An erect, creeping perennial, with tuberous rhizomes and hollow stems; widespread in marshes, the margins of lakes, ponds and rivers, ditches and damp fields, and as a weed; in Ireland it is less restricted to damp ground and is frequently a weed of disturbed and cultivated ground and pastures. It has been used, like several other plants in this family, to staunch bleeding. It has a smell when bruised, but not nearly as strong and unpleasant as that of Hedge Woundwort (p.159).

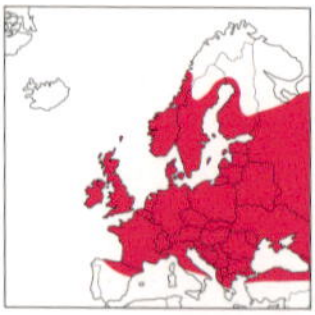

J	F	M	A	M	J
J	A	S	O	N	D

Hedge Woundwort

Stachys sylvatica

ID FACT FILE

Height: 50–120 cm

Flowers: Reddish-purple, with whitish blotches, rarely pink or white. 13–18 mm long, in whorls, forming a dense, pyramidal spike

Leaves: In opposite pairs, oval, stalked, pointed, coarsely toothed

Fruits: 4 nutlets

Lookalikes: Marsh Woundwort (p.158) has solid stems, narrower, unstalked leaves and more pinkish flowers; it is a plant of less shady places.

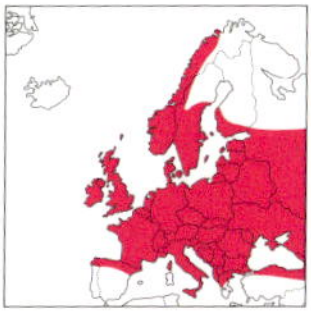

Erect, roughly hairy, unpleasant-smelling perennial, with a creeping rhizome and solid stems; a widespread and common plant of woods, hedges, shady places, abandoned cultivated land and overgrown gardens. The whole plant has a strong smell when bruised or damaged. Nevertheless, it has been used, like several other plants in this family, to staunch bleeding and to heal wounds. This is a characteristic flower of shady places during summer's heat.

J	F	M	A	M	J
J	A	S	O	N	D

Ground-ivy

Glechoma hederacea

ID FACT FILE

Height: 10–50 cm

Flowers: Deep violet, dark-spotted, rarely pink or white, 15–25 mm long, 3–6 in whorls

Leaves: In opposite pairs, heart- or kidney-shaped, stalked, with scalloped margins

Fruits: 4 nutlets

Lookalikes: Self-heal (p.161) has bluish-purple flowers, and blooms later in the year.

Rather slender, softly hairy perennial, sometimes the whole plant tinged purple, with far-creeping, rooting stems; often abundant in woods, hedges and shady banks, also in churchyards, untended gardens and grassy places. Some plants have female as well as hermaphrodite flowers, to encourage cross-pollination. A bitter-tasting plant that was formerly used medicinally and to flavour and preserve beer. This is one of the first flowers of spring, but one which is at its best well into May.

J	F	M	A	M	J
J	A	S	O	N	D

Self-heal

Prunella vulgaris

ID FACT FILE

Height: 5–50 cm

Flowers: Rich bluish-purple, sometimes violet, pink or white, 12–15 mm long, in a dense, cylindrical spike; purplish bracts

Leaves: In opposite pairs, oval, stalked, untoothed or slightly toothed

Fruits: 4 nutlets

Lookalikes: Ground-ivy (p.160) has violet flowers, and blooms earlier in the year; Bugle (p.149) and Skullcap (p.151) have blue flowers.

Hairy, spreading or ascending annual, biennial or short-lived perennial; common in woods, waste places and waysides, damp or dry grassland, on sand-dunes and often in lawns. A very variable species; dwarfed, prostrate plants from lawns keep their features even when grown in good garden soil. The spikes of persistent purplish bracts are distinctive even when the flowers have fallen. The common name reflects a long and useful history of herbal use for staunching and healing wounds.

J	F	M	A	M	J
J	A	S	O	N	D

Marjoram

Origanum vulgare

ID FACT FILE

Height: 20–80 cm

Flowers: Purplish-violet, 4–7 mm long, 2-lipped, in loose heads in a flat-topped cluster; oval, purplish bracts

Leaves: In opposite pairs, oval, stalked, untoothed or shallowly toothed

Fruits: 4 nutlets

Lookalikes: Wild Thyme (p.163) is much smaller; Basil Thyme (*Clinopodium vulgare*) has little smell, and bright purplish-pink flowers about 20 mm long in well-spaced whorls.

Aromatic, hairy, downy perennial, branched above and somewhat woody at the base; common in grassland, scrub and woodland margins on lime-rich soils. It was formerly used to make a tea that was said to cure a number of complaints. Marjoram is still a popular cottage garden plant not only because it is an ornamental and useful herb, but also because the flowers attract numerous feeding butterflies. Mediterranean variants of the plant in gardens have a more pungent smell and flavour.

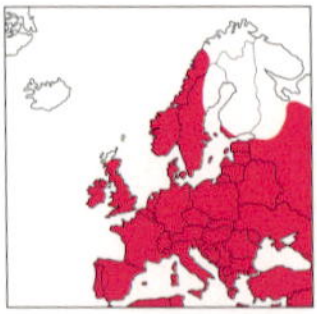

J	F	M	A	M	J
J	A	S	O	N	D

Wild Thyme

Thymus praecox

ID FACT FILE

Height: 5–10 cm

Flowers: Reddish-purple or pink, 3–4 mm long, without upper lip, in spherical flat-topped cluster; purplish calyx

Leaves: In opposite pairs, elliptical or spear-shaped, 4–8 mm, short-stalked

Fruits: 4 nutlets

Lookalikes: Marjoram (p.162) is a much larger plant; Basil Thyme (*Clinopodium vulgare*), also larger, has little smell, and bright purplish-pink flowers about 20 mm long in well-spaced whorls.

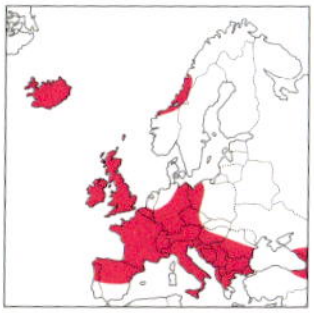

Attractive, often hairy, mat-forming perennial, with a mass of creeping, rooting runners, rather woody at the base, the square stems hairy on two opposite sides. It is a widespread plant of dry or rocky grassland, heaths, sunny banks, cliffs, sand-dunes and sometimes lawns, especially on lime-rich soils and by the sea. Together with Marjoram (p.162), this aromatic plant gives grassland on chalk and limestone much of its characteristic and evocative summertime scent.

J	F	M	A	M	J
J	A	S	O	N	D

Gipsywort

Lycopus europaeus

ID FACT FILE

Height: 30–100 cm

Flowers: Bell-shaped, 3–4 mm long, whitish with purple dots, in wide-spaced whorls; long, hairy calyx; stamens protruding

Leaves: In opposite pairs, spear-shaped, short-stalked, jaggedly toothed, without a smell when bruised

Fruits: 4 nutlets

Lookalikes: Water Mint and Corn Mint (*Mentha arvensis*) (p.165) have larger, lilac flowers; those of Water Mint are mostly in a terminal head, and the leaves are strongly aromatic.

Erect, hairy, mint-like perennial, forming patches by means of a creeping rhizome and runners; a widespread, common and rather conspicuous plant of ditches, margins of ponds, streams, rivers and canals. It is more local in much of N Britain and Ireland. The neatly tiered pairs of opposite leaves give this plant a characteristic appearance. It yields a black dye, the basis of an old and scurrilous rumour of its use by gipsies to dye their hair, to enhance their exotic appearance!

J	F	M	A	M	J
J	A	S	O	N	D

Water Mint

Mentha aquatica

ID FACT FILE

Height: 20–80 cm

Flowers: Lilac, 3–4 mm long, most of them in a terminal head, others in lower, spaced whorls; long, hairy calyx; stamens protruding

Leaves: In opposite pairs, oval, stalked, toothed

Fruits: 4 nutlets

Lookalikes: Corn Mint (*Mentha arvensis*) has paler lilac flowers, all in separate whorls up the stem; it grows in drier places.

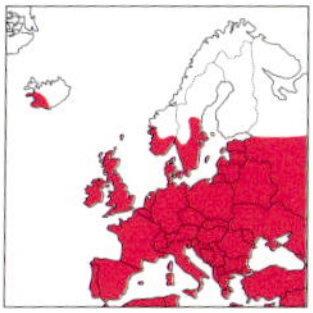

Richly aromatic, hairy, erect perennial of marshes, ditches and the sides of rivers, ponds and lakes. This is the commonest mint of wet places, giving marsh vegetation its characteristic fragrant odour in summer and autumn. Peppermint is a hybrid between Water Mint and garden Spearmint, familiar as the principal ingredient of mint sauce. These and other mints are vigorous plants that frequently escape from gardens to become naturalised in damp or waste places.

J	F	M	A	M	J
J	A	S	O	N	D

Black Nightshade

Solanum nigrum

ID FACT FILE

Height: 10–60 cm

Flowers: White, 5–8 mm across, the petals becoming down-curved, in small, loose clusters; stamens in yellow cone

Leaves: 3–6 cm, stalked, more or less oval or diamond-shaped, usually irregularly toothed, pointed

Fruits: Loose cluster of spherical, shiny black berries

Lookalikes: Deadly Nightshade (*Atropa belladonna*) is a robust perennial, with bell-shaped flowers 2–3 cm long and berries up to 2 cm across, local in woods and scrub on chalk and limestone.

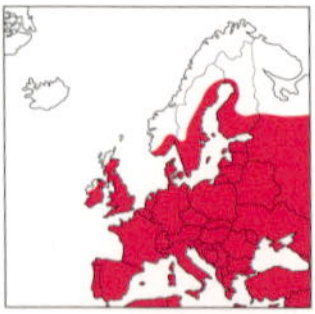

Erect or ascending, branched and often bushy, hairless or downy annual, of arable fields and gardens; widespread in England and Wales but rare in N Britain and Ireland. The lustrous-looking berries, which ripen from green to black during August to October, are poisonous – like those of its cultivated relative, the potato. Although the leaves, too, contain variable amounts of poisonous alkaloids, in S Europe they are sold, cooked and eaten as a green vegetable similar to spinach.

J	F	M	A	M	J
J	A	S	O	N	D

Woody Nightshade

Solanum dulcamara

ID FACT FILE

Height: 50–200 cm, sometimes up to 400 cm

Flowers: Violet, 10–15 mm across, in loose clusters; each petal with 2 green nectary patches at base; stamens in a yellow cone

Leaves: 5–8 cm, the lower 3-lobed, the upper spear-shaped

Fruits: Broadly egg-shaped, scarlet, shiny, translucent berries, c.1 cm long

Lookalikes: Deadly Nightshade (*Atropa belladonna*) is more robust, with bell-shaped flowers and larger, black berries; local in woods and scrub on chalk and limestone.

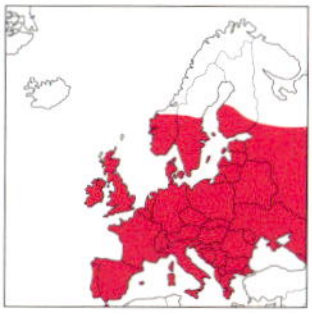

Rather woody, climbing or straggling, downy perennial, of shady places by streams and rivers, hedgerow ditches, overgrown gardens and damp woods. It is a widespread plant, but in Scotland it occurs mainly on the coast and along rivers. It is a characteristic species of swamp woodland, a rare habitat that survives in parts of East Anglia and Ireland; a prostrate, fleshy variant grows on coastal shingle beaches. The plant spreads both by seed and by the production of new shoots from the roots.

J	F	M	A	M	J
J	A	S	O	N	D

Monkey Flower

Mimulus guttatus

ID FACT FILE

HEIGHT: 20–50 cm

FLOWERS: Golden yellow, the throat spotted red, 25–40 mm long, in loose, leafy clusters; glandular-downy calyx

LEAVES: In opposite pairs, broadly oval, irregularly toothed, the upper ones clasping the stem

FRUITS: Oblong capsules c.1 cm long; seeds many

LOOKALIKES: Blood-drop-emlets (*Mimulus luteus*), from Chile, with red-blotched flowers, occurs in similar places, mainly in N Britain.

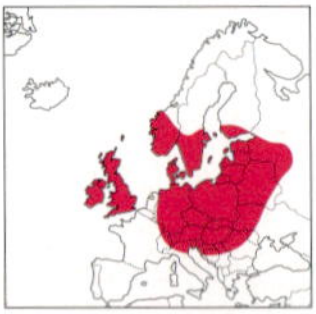

Erect or ascending perennial, with stout, hollow stems that are glandular-downy in the upper part, of stream- and riversides and damp places. Introduced originally from the western USA, it had escaped from gardens by the early 19th century and today it occurs over much of Britain and Ireland, especially in the north; it is rare in East Anglia and the Irish midlands. This attractive plant adds much colour to streamsides and it is often forgotten that it is not a truly native plant.

J	F	M	A	M	J
J	A	S	O	N	D

Great Mullein or Aaron's Rod

Verbascum thapsus

ID FACT FILE

Height: 80–200 cm

Flowers: Pale yellow, 20–50 mm across, in small clusters in the angle of a bract; massed in huge, unbranched spikes

Leaves: Oval or broadly spear-shaped, pointed

Fruits: Egg-shaped capsules containing numerous tiny seeds

Lookalikes: Several other species of mullein occur in similar habitats in Britain, mainly in the south, but not in Ireland.

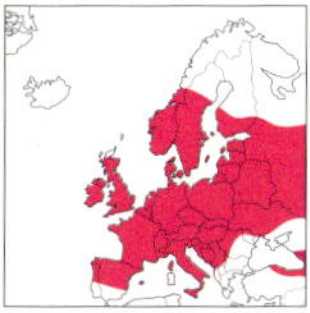

Conspicuous, robust, erect, white-felted biennial, of sunny banks, waste ground, dry roadsides, scrub and wood margins; in Ireland it is often associated with houses or ruins. It is generally a widespread plant, sometimes occurring in crowds, but is rare over much of Ireland and in W and N Scotland. Like other biennials, the young plant develops a rosette of leaves at the end of the first summer, which looks rather like a hairy cabbage. The adult plant can produce many thousands of seeds.

J	F	M	A	M	J
J	A	S	O	N	D

Common Figwort

Scrophularia nodosa

ID FACT FILE

Height: 40–100 cm

Flowers: Helmet-like, 10 mm long, green with a purplish-brown upper lip, in loose, leafy clusters

Leaves: In opposite pairs, oval, short-stalked with cut-off base, double-toothed, pointed

Fruits: Egg-shaped capsules

Lookalikes: Water Figwort (*Scrophularia aquatica*) is taller, with winged stems, blunt leaves and spherical capsules, and grows in wet places.

Erect, hairless perennial, unpleasant-smelling when bruised, with short, thick, knobbly rhizome and square, unwinged stems; of woods, riverbanks and damp, shady places. It is widespread and common through most of Britain and Ireland, although rare in N Scotland. It is not a handsome plant, although a cream-variegated variant finds favour in cottage gardens. However, it has a long history of medicinal use, especially to treat skin complaints and to heal wounds.

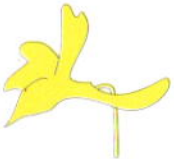

J	F	M	A	M	J
J	A	S	O	N	D

Toadflax

Linaria vulgaris

ID FACT FILE

Height: 30–80 cm

Flowers: Pale yellow, 2–3 cm long, with a dark yellow central patch, in long, fairly loose spikes; long, slender spur

Leaves: Very narrow, spear-shaped, entire, pointed

Fruits: Egg-shaped capsules

Lookalikes: Other snapdragons and toadflaxes, most of them garden escapes, usually have purple or red flowers.

Erect perennial with slender, creeping rhizome; a widespread plant of grassland, hedge-banks and waste land; local in Ireland and N and W Scotland. The long spurs contain nectar; the flowers are pollinated by bees and bumblebees, some of which steal nectar by biting through the spur. This is one of our most handsome wild flowers and a feature of the late summer countryside. The first half of the scientific name denotes the similarity of the leaves to those of flax (Latin: *linum*).

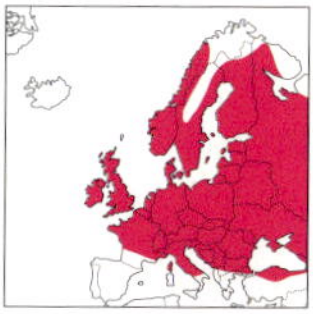

J	F	M	A	M	J
J	A	S	O	N	D

Ivy-leaved Toadflax

Cymbalaria muralis

Hairless, often purplish, trailing perennial, characteristically on walls, but sometimes on rocks, stony ground and even shingle beaches. Originally a native of Italy and adjacent parts of the Alps, it has escaped from gardens throughout W Europe and has been known in Britain since 1640. It now occurs almost throughout Britain and Ireland. The stalks of the capsules grow away from the light, curving downwards as the seeds ripen, and pushing the fruits into chinks and crannies, where the seedlings are better able to establish and grow.

ID FACT FILE

Height: 10–60 cm

Flowers: Snap-dragon-like, lilac, violet or sometimes white, with a yellow central spot, 9–15 mm long, solitary on long stalks

Leaves: Long-stalked, 'ivy'-like, rounded or kidney-shaped, with 5–9 shallow lobes

Fruits: Spherical capsules, on stiff, curved stalks

Lookalikes: None of the other toad-flaxes has the trailing habit of this plant.

J	F	M	A	M	J
J	A	S	O	N	D

Foxglove

Digitalis purpurea

ID FACT FILE

Height: 50–180 cm

Flowers: Broadly tubular, pinkish-purple or reddish-pink, red-spotted and hairy inside, 40–55 mm long, in a long, dense spike

Leaves: Very large, broadly spear-shaped, wrinkled, softly hairy

Fruits: Nearly spherical, downy capsules

Lookalikes: Unlikely to be confused with any other wild plant.

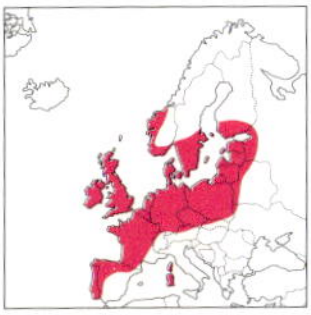

Conspicuous, erect, unbranched, greyish-downy biennial or short-lived perennial; widespread and sometimes abundant in open woods, scrub, heaths and banks on acid soils. Where ground has been cleared or burned, huge numbers may colour the whole landscape, as on new road-verges in Wales and other parts of W Britain. This very poisonous plant yields the drug digitalin, which has long been used in medicine to slow the pace of the heart-beat. The flowers are much visited by bumblebees.

J	F	M	A	M	J
J	A	S	O	N	D

Brooklime

Veronica beccabunga

Somewhat fleshy, hairless perennial, with far-creeping, rooting, sprawling or ascending, hollow stems; common in wet places, ditches and streams, it is widespread in Britain and Ireland, although local in C and W Scotland. The leaves have a sharp taste and have been used as a salad. The blue flowers with a minute tube and only two stamens identify Brooklime as one of the speedwells; it belongs to a group of four similar perennial speedwells that occur in wet or marshy ground.

ID FACT FILE

Height: 20–50 cm

Flowers: Blue, rarely pink, almost flat, 4-lobed, 5–8 mm across, in paired, conical spikes arising from each leaf-pair; 2 stamens

Leaves: In opposite pairs, oval to oblong, short-stalked, shallowly toothed, blunt

Fruits: Flattened capsules, splitting into 4 segments

Lookalikes: Blue Water-speedwell (*Veronica anagallis-aquatica*) has broadly spear-shaped, pointed leaves and paler blue flowers.

J	F	M	A	M	J
J	A	S	O	N	D

Germander Speedwell, or Bird's-eye

Veronica chamaedrys

ID FACT FILE

Height: 10–30 cm

Flowers: Intense blue with a white eye, rarely lilac, c.1 cm across, in loose conical clusters of 10–20; 2 stamens

Leaves: In opposite pairs, oval-triangular, toothed

Fruits: Heart-shaped, hairy capsules, splitting into 2 segments

Lookalikes: Heath Speedwell (*Veronica officinalis*) has stems that are hairy all round and bluish-lilac flowers in dense clusters; it grows in dry grassland and on heaths.

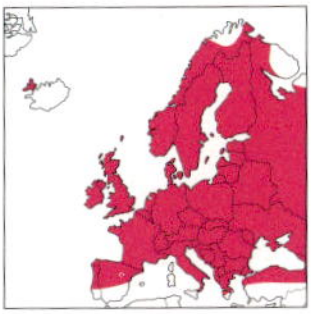

Hairy perennial, with far-creeping, rooting, ascending stems with two opposite lines of white hairs; a common plant of wood margins and grassland, it occurs throughout Britain and Ireland, and is rare only in the Outer Hebrides and Orkney. This is one of the most elegant and attractive of all our wild flowers. Alas, the delicate petals fall easily, especially if the plant is picked: perhaps the origin of a superstition that harm will come to the eyes of the picker or of his or her mother.

J	F	M	A	M	J
J	A	S	O	N	D

All through mild winters.

Common Field-speedwell

Veronica persica

ID FACT FILE

Height: 10–50 cm

Flowers: Blue, with darker bluish-violet veins, white markings and eye, 8–12 mm across, solitary on slender stalks; 2 stamens

Leaves: In opposite pairs, short-stalked, oval or triangular, coarsely toothed

Fruits: Sticky-hairy capsules with 2 divergent lobes

Lookalikes: Ivy-leaved Speedwell (*Veronica hederifolia*), with 3- to 5-lobed leaves, smaller, lilac or blue flowers, and stout, rounded fruits, grows in gardens and woods.

Prostrate or spreading, hairy annual of disturbed ground, especially good, cultivated soil. Although it arrived in Britain from SW Asia only in the early 19th century, it is now the commonest speedwell of cultivated land. These comprise a group of eight, all annuals, some of them now rare as a result of modern intensive agriculture. Common Field-speedwell, alone of the group, is one of our most successful weeds and can cause severe infestations of vegetable crops, allotments and gardens.

J	F	M	A	M	J
J	A	S	O	N	D

Slender Speedwell

Veronica filiformis

ID FACT FILE

Height: 5–20 cm

Flowers: Pale blue, with a white eye and lilac veins, 10–15 mm across, solitary, on long, slender stalks; 2 stamens

Leaves: In opposite pairs, kidney-shaped, rounded-toothed, blunt

Fruits: Capsules rarely formed in N Europe

Lookalikes: Thyme-leaved Speedwell (*Veronica serpyllifolia*) is a native plant of grassland, with more or less untoothed leaves and pale blue or whitish flowers in loose spikes.

Slender, mat-forming, creeping perennial, the stems rooting at the nodes, spreading rapidly in damp grassland, riverbanks, churchyards and lawns. Introduced from the Caucasus in 1808 as a garden plant, it soon escaped into the wild. It does not set seed in Britain and Ireland, but rooting fragments are spread by mowing and other disturbance. This most elegant of wild flowers locally imparts a striking, blue shimmer to grassy places and lawns in early May. It is a worthy addition to our flora.

J	F	M	A	M	J
J	A	S	O	N	D

Common Cow-wheat

Melampyrum pratense

ID FACT FILE

Height: 20–60 cm

Flowers: Yellowish-white or yellow, 10–18 mm long, in pairs, turned to the same side; leaf-like, slightly toothed bracts

Leaves: In opposite pairs, rather narrow, oval or spear-shaped, pointed

Fruits: 4-seeded capsules

Lookalikes: Yellow-rattle (p.179) has toothed leaves and yellowish-green bracts; it occurs in grassland.

A slender, branched, mostly hairless annual of dry woods, scrub, heaths and grassland on acid soils. It is widespread in the British Isles, although local in E England and much of Ireland. A very variable species: plants on moors sometimes have pinkish-purple flowers and another striking variant has golden-yellow flowers. Like the eyebrights and some other members of the family, Common Cow-wheat is a semi-parasite, taking water and minerals from the roots of other plants.

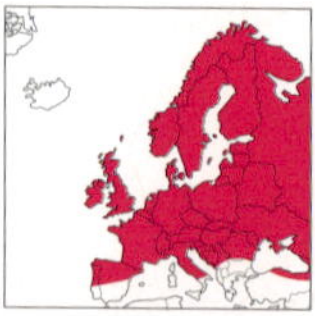

J	F	M	A	M	J
J	A	S	O	N	D

Yellow-rattle

Rhinanthus minor

Erect, rather stiff, more or less hairless annual of grassland, especially in damper places and in the west. It is a classic wild flower of old meadows, and is sadly now greatly reduced in abundance by modern agriculture. Like the eyebrights, louseworts and some other members of the family, Yellow-rattle is a semi-parasite, taking water and minerals from the roots of other plants. The name derives from the rattling of the ripe seeds within the dried-out, inflated calyx. A variable species.

ID FACT FILE

Height: 10–50 cm

Flowers: Yellow, with 2 short, violet teeth, 12–15 mm long, in loose spikes; calyx inflated and persistent in fruit; conspicuous, yellowish-green bracts

Leaves: In opposite pairs, narrow, oblong or spear-shaped, toothed, pointed

Fruits: Capsules, each within inflated calyx; seeds flat, winged

Lookalikes: Common Cow-wheat (p.178) has untoothed leaves and inconspicuous bracts; it grows mostly in woods and on heaths.

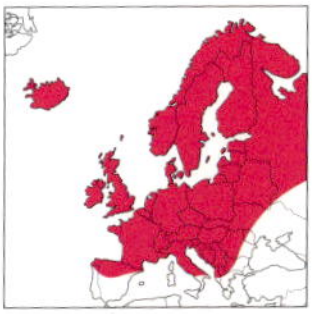

J	F	M	A	M	J
J	A	S	O	N	D

Eyebright

Euphrasia nemorosa

ID FACT FILE

Height: 5–35 cm

Flowers: White, flushed and streaked with yellow and purple, 4–10 mm long, arranged in loose, leafy clusters

Leaves: In opposite pairs, oval-triangular, rounded at the base, jagged-toothed

Fruits: Small, oblong, hairy capsules with many tiny seeds

Lookalikes: Some 30 closely related species of eyebright occur in Britain and Ireland.

Elegant, often branched, dark green, hairy or sticky-hairy annual, of grassland, heaths and sand-dunes throughout Britain and Ireland. Like Yellow-rattle and some other members of the family, Eyebright is a semi-parasite, taking water and minerals from the roots of other plants. Eyebright belongs to a very variable group of many closely related 'microspecies' and hybrids, several of them restricted to Britain. It has a long history as a herbal treatment for minor eye complaints.

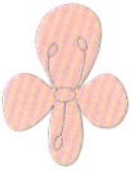

J	F	M	A	M	J
J	A	S	O	N	D

Lousewort

Pedicularis sylvatica

A tufted perennial that is a widespread and locally common plant of moors, heaths and bogs, although scarce in C England and East Anglia. Like the yellow-rattles, eyebrights, and some other members of the family, Lousewort is a semi-parasite, taking water and minerals from the roots of other plants. Plants from Ireland and a few places in W Wales have a hairy calyx. The plant's common name refers to 'lice' or liver-flukes, which can infest animals in the wet pastures in which the plant grows.

ID FACT FILE

Height: 5–25 cm

Flowers: Reddish- or purplish-pink, 15–25 mm long, in short, loose spikes; hairless or hairy, papery calyx

Leaves: Spear-shaped, deeply lobed

Fruits: Curved capsules within persistent, inflated calyx

Lookalikes: Marsh Lousewort or Red Rattle (*Pedicularis palustris*) is a biennial up to 50 cm tall with a single, branched stem and downy calyx, of damp grassland and heaths, usually on acid soils.

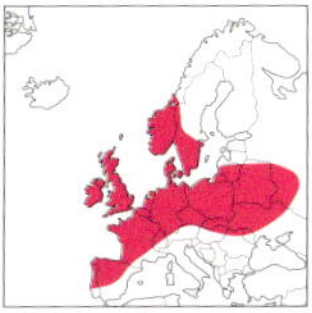

J	F	M	A	M	J
J	A	S	O	N	D

Common Broomrape

Orobanche minor

ID FACT FILE

Height: 10–80 cm

Flowers: Corolla 5-lobed, yellowish, tinged violet, pink or purple, 10–15 mm long, in a loose, cylindrical spike

Leaves: Scale-like

Fruits: Cylindrical capsules, containing many dust-like seeds

Lookalikes: The commonest of 12 native species of broomrape. The closely related Toothwort (*Lathraea squamaria*), with 1-sided clusters of whitish or pink flowers, is a rather scarce plant, parasitic on Hazel and Elm.

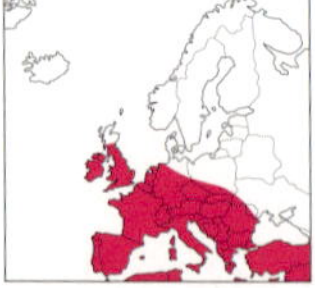

Erect, fleshy, sticky-hairy, yellow, brownish, pink or purplish perennial, superficially resembling an orchid. Often erratic in appearance, it is widespread but local in dry grassland, less often in gardens. This plant produces no green chlorophyll and is parasitic on the roots of numerous plants, especially members of the clover and daisy families, including garden plants. From these it extracts water, minerals and sugars to sustain its own growth, flowering and seed production.

J	F	M	A	M	J
J	A	S	O	N	D

Common Butterwort

Pinguicula vulgaris

ID FACT FILE

Height: 5–10 cm, sometimes up to 18 cm

Flowers: Violet, usually with a white throat, 10–15 mm long, solitary on long stems; straight spur, 4–6 mm

Leaves: All in a basal rosette, oval or oblong, pale or yellowish-green, very sticky above

Fruits: Egg-shaped capsules, containing many small seeds

Lookalikes: Pale Butterwort (*Pinguicula lusitanica*), with smaller, lilac flowers, the spur 2–4 mm, down-curved, is locally common in W Britain and W Ireland.

An attractive, distinctive, tufted perennial, with the remarkable ability to entrap, digest and absorb small insects to supplement its nutrient requirements. It is a plant of bogs, wet moors and heaths, and wet rocks and grassland, including old meadows. It occurs throughout Britain and Ireland, but is rare in S and E England. The trapping of insects is a nutritional adaptation to low mineral levels in boggy habitats, one shared with plants in the sundew family (p.58).

J	F	M	A	M	J
J	A	S	O	N	D

Greater Plantain

Plantago major

ID FACT FILE

Height: 5–40 cm, sometimes up to 60 cm

Flowers: Small, yellowish-green, in a dense, cylindrical spike; stamens lilac, fading to yellowish

Leaves: Oval or elliptical, usually with 5–9 parallel veins, stalked, generally tough and hairless, sometimes very large

Fruits: Egg-shaped capsules, opening by a lid; usually 8–12 seeds

Lookalikes: Ribwort Plantain (*Plantago lanceolata*) has spear-shaped leaves, narrowly egg-shaped flower-spikes and yellow stamens.

A tufted perennial, with rosettes of leathery leaves and fibrous stems that are well able to withstand trampling; abundant in grassy places and waysides, and on waste ground, especially by paths and gates. A variable species; plants from cultivated land and lake shores have pale green, hairy leaves with 3–5 veins and up to 30 seeds in each capsule. They are regarded as a distinct subspecies. The leaves were once used to dress wounds, and the plant has healing and soothing properties.

J	F	M	A	M	J
J	A	S	O	N	D

Honeysuckle

Lonicera periclymenum

ID FACT FILE

Height: 2–6 m

Flowers: Tubular, 2-lipped, 3–5 cm long, yellowish-cream tinged lilac or reddish, fading to orange, richly scented, in clusters

Leaves: In opposite pairs, oval, very short-stalked, downy, slightly paler beneath

Fruits: Clusters of shiny red berries

Lookalikes: Other honeysuckles sometimes escape from gardens, especially Perfoliate Honeysuckle (*Lonicera caprifolium*), which has fused pairs of leaves.

A woody climber, twining (clockwise) in hedges and amongst the branches of trees and shrubs, or near the ground in coastal heathland, very conspicuous when in flower. A familiar and much-loved wild flower that is renowned for its scent, especially at night, when the flowers are visited by moths. It is the food plant of the caterpillars of the White Admiral butterfly. The new leaves are one of the first signs of green in woodlands during late winter. The berries are poisonous.

J	F	M	A	M	J
J	A	S	O	N	D

Moschatel or Townhall Clock

Adoxa moschatellina

ID FACT FILE

Height: 5–10 cm

Flowers: Yellowish-green, usually 5, in a compact head 6–8 mm across; uppermost one with 4 petals and stamens, the others with 5; stamens pale yellow

Leaves: Long-stalked, somewhat fleshy, 3-lobed, the lobes further divided into rounded lobes

Fruits: Small, green, fleshy drupes

Lookalikes: The young leaves may be mistaken for those of Wood Anemone (p.34), in which the basal leaves appear after flowering.

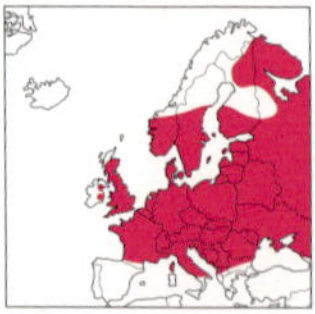

A delicate, pale green, hairless perennial, forming patches up to several metres across; locally common in woods, hedges and damp, shady places. It occurs throughout Britain, northwards to the Cromarty Firth, but has only two Irish stations. When the plant is wet it smells faintly of musk. Moschatel is the only species in its family. The seeds are said to be dispersed by snails. The arrangement of the flowers, facing outwards or upwards, gives the plant the local name of Townhall Clock.

J	F	M	A	M	J
J	A	S	O	N	D

Common Cornsalad

Valerianella locusta

ID FACT FILE

Height: 5–20 cm, sometimes up to 40 cm

Flowers: Pale lilac, 1–2 mm across, funnel-shaped, in paired, dense, rather flat-topped clusters 1–2 cm across

Leaves: In opposite pairs, spoon-shaped; the upper more oblong, slightly toothed

Fruits: 2–3 mm long, green, 1-seeded, swollen but flattened, in dense clusters

Lookalikes: The 5 species of cornsalad are difficult to distinguish apart.

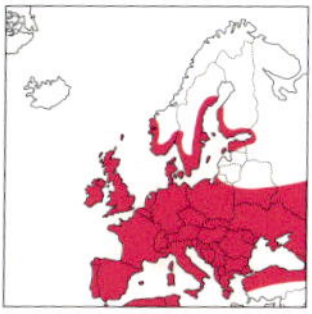

Slender, erect annual of cultivated land, dry banks, walls, rock outcrops and sand-dunes. A variable species: very compact, dwarf plants are sometimes found on sand-dunes. A robust, cultivated variant of this plant (Cornsalad or Mache) is grown in gardens and as a commercial salad crop. This is the only one of our five species of cornsalad, all plants of similar open and disturbed habitats, that is at all widespread. All have declined in the face of modern intensive agriculture.

J	F	M	A	M	J
J	A	S	O	N	D

Common Valerian

Valeriana officinalis

ID FACT FILE

Height: 50–150 cm

Flowers: Pale pink or white, 5 mm across, tubular with a pouch-like spur, scented, densely grouped in a flat head; 3 stamens

Leaves: In opposite pairs, compound, or very deeply lobed, the margins toothed

Fruits: 1-seeded, 2–5 mm, with a crown of hairs

Lookalikes: Red Valerian (p.189) has a longer-spurred corolla that is usually red; Marsh Valerian (*Valeriana dioica*), a smaller plant with less divided leaves, occurs in marshes northwards to C Scotland.

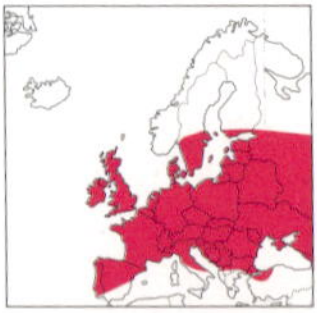

Robust, erect, rather hairy perennial of damp and dry grassland, scrub and open woods, widespread throughout Britain and Ireland. This and other species of valerian have a curious, rather unpleasant, but characteristic smell; the root is said to be irresistible to cats. An extract from the plant has been used medicinally as a sedative – hence the scientific name (Latin: *valere*, to heal) – and 'Valerian drops' feature as a poison in old-fashioned crime stories.

J	F	M	A	M	J
J	A	S	O	N	D

Red, or Spur, Valerian

Centranthus ruber

ID FACT FILE

Height: 30–80 cm

Flowers: Mostly red, but often pink or white, 5 mm across, tubular with a slender spur, scented, in branched clusters grouped in a pyramidal head; 1 stamen

Leaves: In opposite pairs, broadly spear-shaped, usually untoothed, pointed

Fruits: 1-seeded, crowned with a feathery plume

Lookalikes: Common Valerian (p.188) has a shorter, pink or white corolla, with a short, pouch-like spur.

A striking, somewhat bluish-green, hairless, ascending or erect perennial, rather woody at the base; locally common on walls, old buildings, rocks, cliffs, road and railway cuttings, waste places and gardens. Although well-established, like the Wallflower (p.50) this plant is introduced from S Europe via gardens; at one time it was widely planted on cuttings of new roads. It is still spreading, but remains rare over much of N Britain, and the midlands and the north of Ireland.

J	F	M	A	M	J
J	A	S	O	N	D

Teasel

Dipsacus fullonum

ID FACT FILE

Height: 50–200 cm, sometimes up to 300 cm

Flowers: Violet, in an egg-shaped head 3–9 cm long; basket of 8–12 bracts, narrow, upward-curved, spiny, as long as the flowerhead

Leaves: In opposite, fused pairs, spear-shaped, prickly beneath

Fruits: 1-seeded, massed in characteristic heads

Lookalikes: A distinctive plant; two other teasels are smaller and much rarer.

A stately, robust, hairless, erect biennial of streamsides, damp, grassy places, waysides and waste ground. It is widespread in S Britain, extending northwards to Fife, but rare in the north and in Ireland. The cups formed by the bases of the fused leaves fill with rain and dew, drowning many insects. A distinct subspecies with downcurved bracts, Fuller's Teasel, has long been used to raise the nap or pile of woollen cloth. A crop is still grown near Taunton in Somerset for this purpose.

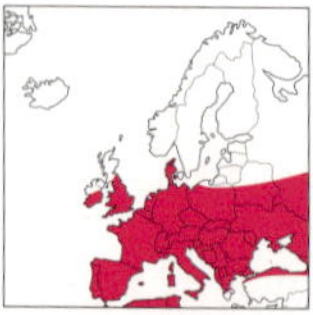

J	F	M	A	M	J
J	A	S	O	N	D

Devil's-bit Scabious

Succisa pratensis

ID FACT FILE

Height: 20–100 cm

Flowers: Dark bluish-purple, rarely pink or white; corolla 4-lobed, the outer lobes larger than the inner, in a long-stalked, domed head 18–25 mm across

Leaves: Basal leaves in a rosette; stem leaves in opposite pairs, elliptical, the upper ones narrower

Fruits: 1-seeded, c.5 mm

Lookalikes: Field Scabious (p.192) and Small Scabious (p.192, Lookalikes) have lilac flowers in heads more than 25 mm across.

Erect perennial of damp grassland and marshes. It can be very abundant and ubiquitous in grassland and grassy coastal heathland, as over large areas of W Ireland. The short, thick rhizome has an abruptly cut-off end – bitten off by the devil! This is the food plant of the caterpillar of the rare, declining Marsh Fritillary butterfly. The word scabious derives from the former herbal use of this and related plants to cure scabies and other unpleasant skin complaints.

J	F	M	A	M	J
J	A	S	O	N	D

Field Scabious

Knautia arvensis

ID FACT FILE

Height: 30–100 cm

Flowers: Lilac, rarely white; corolla 4-lobed, the outer lobes larger than the inner, in a long-stalked, flat head 25–40 mm across

Leaves: In opposite pairs, the lower entire, the upper deeply lobed

Fruits: 1-seeded, 5–6 mm long

Lookalikes: Small Scabious (*Scabiosa columbaria*) is shorter, with smaller flower-heads and 5-lobed corollas; it occurs on grassland on lime-rich soils.

Erect, hairy biennial or perennial of grassland, dry banks and road-verges; formerly on cultivated land. It is widespread, although rare in W and N Scotland and much of W Ireland. The word Scabious derives from the use of this group of plants to cure scabies and other skin complaints; today they are prized more for ornament, both as wild flowers and in gardens. Britain's native scabious species are all important food plants for the caterpillar of the Chalkhill Blue butterfly.

J	F	M	A	M	J
J	A	S	O	N	D

Giant Bellflower

Campanula latifolia

ID FACT FILE

Height: 50–150 cm

Flowers: Blue or violet-blue, bell-shaped, 40–55 mm long, in a long, leafy spike; narrow calyx-teeth up to 5 cm long

Leaves: Oval, irregularly toothed, stalked; the upper narrower, stalkless

Fruits: Dome-shaped capsules, with many tiny seeds

Lookalikes: Nettle-leaved Bellflower (*Campanula trachelium*) is hairier, has triangular leaves and darker blue flowers and is more southerly in distribution, and also occurs in SE Ireland.

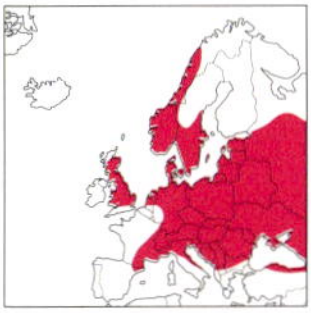

Stately, robust, erect perennial of woods, hedges, shady places and streamsides; locally common in Scotland and N England, but absent from S England and in Ireland only naturalised here and there in the north. A very striking and characteristic wild plant in some areas such as the limestone dales of the West Riding of Yorkshire, it is cultivated for ornament and the young shoots can be cooked and eaten like spinach. *Campanula* (Latin: little bell) denotes the shape of the flowers.

J	F	M	A	M	J
J	A	S	O	N	D

Creeping Bellflower

Campanula rapunculoides

ID FACT FILE

Height: 40–100 cm

Flowers: Violet-blue, narrowly bell-shaped, 2–3 cm long, in a long, 1-sided, showy spike; calyx-teeth bent back at flowering

Leaves: Oval, toothed, stalked; the upper narrower, stalkless

Fruits: Dome-shaped capsules, with many tiny seeds

Lookalikes: Clustered Bellflower (*Campanula glomerata*), shorter, with flowers mostly in a terminal cluster, is locally common in grassland on lime-rich soils in England, S Wales and E Scotland.

Erect, downy or hairless perennial, the creeping roots giving rise to clumps, a plant of hedges, scrub, grassland and road-verges; also a garden weed. It is scattered throughout Britain, except N Scotland and SW England, and in Ireland mostly near the E coast. Widespread as a wild plant over most of N Europe, it was introduced to gardens in Britain and Ireland, whence it has escaped to become naturalised. The whitish, tuberous roots have been used as a vegetable.

J	F	M	A	M	J
J	A	S	O	N	D

Harebell

Campanula rotundifolia

ID FACT FILE

Height: 10–50 cm

Flowers: Violet-blue, bell-shaped, 12–20 mm long, nodding, in open, loose, branched clusters; very narrow, pointed calyx-teeth

Leaves: Lower ones heart-shaped, rounded, toothed, stalked; upper spear-shaped, slightly toothed

Fruits: Broadly conical capsules, with many tiny seeds, nodding when ripe

Lookalikes: Other bellflowers are more robust and less elegant and delicate.

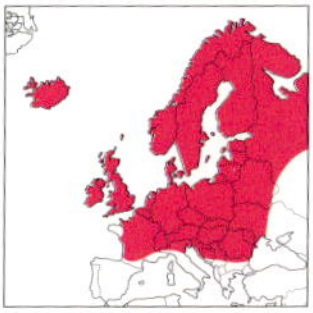

Slender, erect or ascending, little-branched, hairless, creeping perennial of dry grassland, hedge-banks, heaths, rocky ground and sand-dunes. It exudes a white, milky juice when cut. This plant is the Bluebell of Scotland, where the English Bluebell (p.237) is known as Wild Hyacinth. A variable species that needs more study; the rather fine-looking plants that occur on and near western coasts have fewer, slightly larger flowers and are regarded by some botanists as a separate species.

J	F	M	A	M	J
J	A	S	O	N	D

Sheep's-bit

Jasione montana

ID FACT FILE

Height: 10–50 cm

Flowers: Blue, c.5 mm long, 5-lobed, in a long-stalked, hemispherical head 10–25 mm across; oval or triangular bracts

Leaves: Narrowly oblong or spear-shaped, with untoothed or slightly toothed, wavy margin

Fruits: Egg-shaped capsules

Lookalikes: Field Scabious and Small Scabious (p.192) have lilac flowers in flat heads usually more than 25 mm across; Devil's-bit Scabious (p.191) is a taller, more robust plant with larger, bluish-purple flowers.

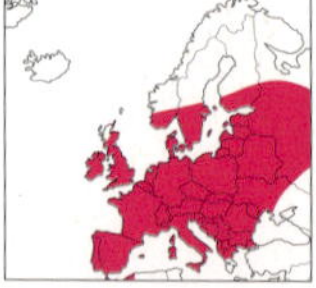

Hairy, erect or ascending, annual, biennial or short-lived perennial; widespread on heaths, dry banks, rocks and cliffs, mostly on acid, sandy or stony soils. Plants from cliffs and walls near the sea on western coasts are more robust and have flowers 20–35 mm across. This scabious-like plant can be distinguished from the true scabious species (pp.191–2) by the stamens, which do not protrude from the flowers (see also Lookalikes). Blue is an uncommon colour among our native wild flowers.

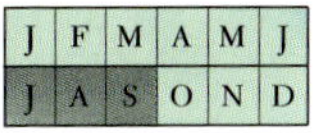

Hemp Agrimony

Eupatorium cannabinum

ID FACT FILE

Height: 30–180 cm

Flowers: Pink or reddish-lilac, 5–6 in heads 3–5 mm across, without ray florets, in branched, flat-topped clusters

Leaves: In opposite pairs, 3- to 5-lobed, the lobes spear-shaped, toothed, the central ones longer

Fruits: Heads of 1-seeded fruits, each with a 'parachute' of white hairs

Lookalikes: The plant bears a superficial resemblance to Common Valerian (p.188), which has compound or deeply lobed leaves.

Erect, robust, leafy, downy perennial, with reddish stems, forming clumps in wet woods, marshes, hedgerows, damp, grassy places and scrub, sometimes on shingle beaches or amongst limestone rocks. A widespread plant, but mostly coastal in Scotland; local in Ireland, where a dwarf variant occurs in the Burren of Co. Clare. The second half of the scientific name reflects the similarity of the leaves to those of Hemp (*Cannabis sativa*), related to Hop (p.11, Lookalikes).

J	F	M	A	M	J
J	A	S	O	N	D

Golden-rod

Solidago virgaurea

ID FACT FILE

Height: 20–180 cm

Flowers: In heads 3–5 mm across, without ray florets, massed in branched spikes

Leaves: Dark green, somewhat leathery; lower leaves in a loose rosette, spoon-shaped; stem leaves spear-shaped, narrower

Fruits: Heads of 1-seeded fruits, each with a crown of brownish hairs

Lookalikes: Garden Golden-rod (*Solidago altissima*), which is taller, with many tiny heads of flowers in dense, 1-sided clusters, often escapes.

Erect, little-branched, somewhat downy perennial of dry, open woods, heaths, hedge-banks and rocky ground, especially on well-drained, acid soils. It is widespread, but local in both the Irish and English midlands and in East Anglia. An infusion of this plant has been used for its healing properties. A very variable species: for example plants from the Burren of Co. Clare are dwarf and flower in June–July, whereas most plants are tall and flower in August–September.

J	F	M	A	M	J
J	A	S	O	N	D

All through mild winters.

Daisy

Bellis perennis

ID FACT FILE

Height: 5–20 cm

Flowers: Solitary heads 1–3 cm across, the disc florets yellow, the ray florets white, reddish or purplish below

Leaves: All basal, spoon-shaped, stalked, bluntly toothed, slightly fleshy and leathery

Fruits: Head of 1-seeded fruits, all without hairs

Lookalikes: Ox-eye Daisy (p.211), with which it often grows, is a very much larger and more robust plant than even cultivated daisies.

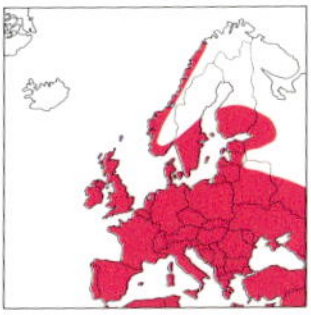

A tufted, downy perennial with erect stems. This familiar and almost ubiquitous wild flower is most closely associated with closely mown grass: even a small, urban lawn will have a few Daisies. The plant's native habitat of old, short grassland is now much reduced, although fine stands of Daisies can still be seen on seaside banks, or grazed hedge-banks inland, and in churchyards. Larger variants are grown in gardens. The flowers close in the evening and on dull or wet days.

J	F	M	A	M	J
J	A	S	O	N	D

Sea Aster

Aster tripolium

Erect, fleshy annual, biennial or perennial; an abundant plant of saltmarshes all around the coasts of Britain and Ireland, together with the banks of tidal rivers; also on sea-cliffs and rocks in the west, and in a few saline marshes in the W Midlands of England. The flowers of many plants in some parts of England – for example the Thames Estuary – lack ray florets. This plant was grown in gardens before the Michaelmas Daisy was introduced from N America in the 17th century.

ID FACT FILE

Height: 20–80 cm, sometimes up to 150 cm

Flowers: Heads 10–25 mm across, the disc florets yellow, ray florets 10–30, mauve or lilac (or absent), in loose clusters

Leaves: Spear-shaped, usually untoothed

Fruits: Heads of 1-seeded fruits, each with a 'parachute' of whitish hairs

Lookalikes: Michaelmas Daisy (*Aster novae-belgii*) frequently escapes from gardens; it is taller, not fleshy, and forms clumps on waste ground and railway embankments.

J	F	M	A	M	J
J	A	S	O	N	D

Canadian Fleabane

Conyza canadensis

ID FACT FILE

Height: 30–180 cm

Flowers: Heads 3–5 mm across, with white or pinkish disc and ray florets, numerous in long, branched loose clusters

Leaves: Narrow, spear-shaped, untoothed or finely toothed

Fruits: Heads of 1-seeded fruits, each with a 'parachute' of hairs

Lookalikes: The cudweeds are all much smaller, white-woolly annuals; Marsh Cudweed (p.203) has flowers in flat-topped clusters.

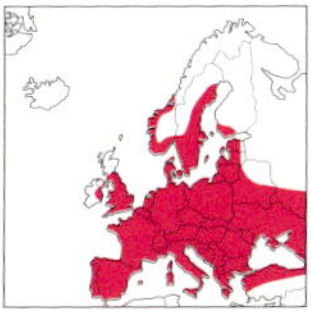

Erect, branched, leafy, pale green, hairy annual of waste ground, derelict land, fallow fields and sand-dunes. An early arrival from N America in the 17th century, it is today especially common in SC and SE England, and has long been a feature of waste ground in and around London. In the 1980s it was reported in Ireland, from Dublin. It may spread on farmland set aside under EU rules, and further expansion of its range is likely should global warming modify our climate.

J	F	M	A	M	J
J	A	S	O	N	D

Common Fleabane

Pulicaria dysenterica

ID FACT FILE

Height: 20–60 cm

Flowers: Heads 15–30 mm across, the disc and ray florets golden yellow, numerous in loose, flat-topped clusters

Leaves: Oblong or spear-shaped, wrinkled, remotely toothed

Fruits: Heads of 1-seeded fruits, the inner ones with a 'parachute' of hairs

Lookalikes: Elecampane (*Inula helenium*), a more robust plant up to 1 m tall with flowerheads 5–8 cm across, is an ancient medicinal herb usually found near houses and ruins.

Erect, branched, rather hairy perennial with creeping runners, forming large patches in marshes, ditches, damp hollows and wet fields. It often occurs in grazed or disturbed, damp grassland, especially on clay soils. Geoffrey Grigson described the plant succinctly in his book *The Englishman's Flora* as: 'The yellow 'daisy' of the wide, damp, rushy road-verges.' It is commonest in S England, becoming rarer further north: it is rare in N Scotland, but widespread in Ireland.

J	F	M	A	M	J
J	A	S	O	N	D

Marsh Cudweed

Filaginella uliginosa

ID FACT FILE

Height: 5–20 cm

Flowers: Heads 3–4 mm across, disc and ray florets yellowish-brown, 3–10 in dense clusters, surrounded by pale brown bracts and bract-like leaves

Leaves: Narrow, oblong or spoon-shaped, up to 5 cm long, untoothed or sometimes slightly toothed, densely woolly-hairy

Fruits: Heads of 1-seeded fruits, each with a 'parachute' of hairs

Lookalikes: One of the commonest of several species of cudweed, a complex group that appeals only to the dedicated botanist.

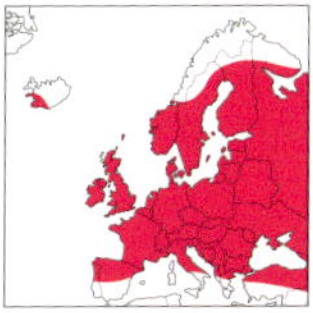

A tufted, branched, spreading or ascending, pale grey-woolly annual of open, damp ground, marshes and heaths, especially on disturbed ground and paths where it can be quite abundant. It is widespread in Britain and Ireland. John Gerard in his 1597 *Herball* gave a charming explanation of why the plant was known in Scotland as 'Son-afore-the-father': 'bicause the yonger, or those flowers that spring up later, are higher, and over top those that come first, as many wicked children do unto their parents!'

J	F	M	A	M	J
J	A	S	O	N	D

Trifid Bur-marigold

Bidens tripartita

ID FACT FILE

Height: 20–60 cm

Flowers: Heads 10–25 mm across, disc florets yellow, ray florets usually absent, in branched clusters with 5–8 leaf-like bracts

Leaves: In opposite pairs, 3-lobed (rarely 5-lobed), the lobes spear-shaped, coarsely toothed

Fruits: Heads of flattened, wedge-shaped, 1-seeded fruits, each with down-turned marginal hairs and 3–4 barbed bristles

Lookalikes: Nodding Bur-marigold (*Bidens cernua*) has spear-shaped leaves and nodding flowerheads.

A rather dowdy, erect, branched, often hairy annual, with purplish, winged stems, that occurs on the margins or dried mud of lakes, ponds and rivers, ditches and in damp waste places. Often growing in great, dense crowds, it is generally widespread, but is rare north of Cumbria and Galway Bay. The bristly fruits adhere readily and firmly to clothing (especially woolly socks) and fur, which serves to disperse the seeds most effectively. Very rarely, flowerheads have yellow ray florets.

J	F	M	A	M	J
J	A	S	O	N	D

Gallant Soldier

Galinsoga parviflora

ID FACT FILE

Height: 10–80 cm

Flowers: Heads of yellow florets 3–5 mm across, each with 5 (sometimes 4 or 6) small, white ray florets

Leaves: In opposite pairs, oval, with a few large, marginal teeth

Fruits: Tiny, oval, flattened, black, with minute hairs and a tuft of scales at one end

Lookalikes: Hairy Gallant Soldier (*Galinsoga quadriradiata*), another, but less common, introduced weed from S America, has densely hairy stems.

Almost hairless, branched annual of cultivated land; sometimes abundant in gardens, allotments, nursery beds and vegetable crops, especially in SE England. Introduced from Peru, it escaped from Kew Gardens during the 1860s and spread through much of Britain; during the 1980s it was reported from Ireland. It is an interesting example of a plant that acquired a popular name within a few years of its arrival here. Tiny bristles on the fruit, which readily adhere to clothing or fur, aid seed dispersal.

J	F	M	A	M	J
J	A	S	O	N	D

Scentless Mayweed

Matricaria perforata

ID FACT FILE

Height: 10–80 cm

Flowers: Heads 30–45 mm in diameter, with yellow disc florets and white ray florets, solitary or in very loose clusters

Leaves: Compound, feathery, with numerous narrow segments

Fruits: Heads of 1-seeded, minutely ribbed fruits, without hairs

Lookalikes: The mayweeds are difficult to distinguish. Chamomile (*Chamaemelum nobile*), a decreasing plant of inland and coastal heaths (and popular in gardens), is a mat-forming, aromatic perennial with flower-heads 18–25 mm across.

Erect or ascending, much-branched annual of cultivated land, field borders, roadsides and waste ground. A variable species: similar plants from seashores and shingle beaches, with fleshy leaves and slightly larger flowers, are often distinguished as a different species, Sea Mayweed. Although Scentless Mayweed is a common and most successful weed, several other mayweeds have decreased markedly since 1945, as a result of modern intensive farming methods and weed-killers.

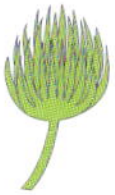

J	F	M	A	M	J
J	A	S	O	N	D

Pineapple Weed

Matricaria discoidea

ID FACT FILE

Height: 5–40 cm

Flowers: Almost spherical heads, 5–9 mm in diameter, of greenish-yellow disc florets; no ray florets

Leaves: Compound, feathery, with numerous narrow segments

Fruits: Heads of 1-seeded fruits, without hairs

Lookalikes: A distinctive plant. Scentless Mayweed (p.206) and other mayweeds have conspicuous white ray florets, giving them a daisy-like appearance.

Erect, stiffly branched, aromatic annual, of pathsides, especially by field gates and other trampled places, waste ground and cultivated land. The whole plant smells strongly of pineapple (some say apple) when bruised. So widely is this undistinguished-looking but successful weed now distributed worldwide that its precise origin (probably western USA) is unknown. First recorded in Britain in 1871, and Ireland in 1894, it spread over much of these islands in the first quarter of this century.

J	F	M	A	M	J
J	A	S	O	N	D

Yarrow

Achillea millefolium

ID FACT FILE

Height: 10–100 cm

Flowers: Heads 3–6 mm across, with white or cream disc florets and 5 white or pinkish-purple ray florets, in flat-topped clusters

Leaves: Fern-like and feathery, with numerous narrow segments

Fruits: Heads of nut-like, 1-seeded fruits, without hairs

Lookalikes: Sneezewort (*Achillea ptarmica*), of damp heaths and marshes, has undivided, toothed leaves, and clusters of flowerheads 12–18 mm across, with greenish disc and white ray florets.

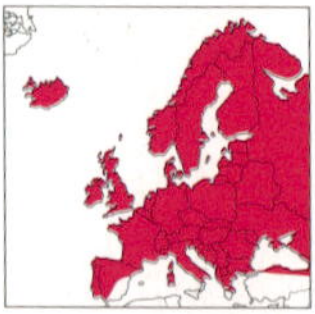

Erect, tough-stemmed, hairy, aromatic perennial, forming clumps and patches; a common plant of dry grassland, hedge-banks and waste places, a prominent feature of village greens, roadsides and untended lawns in late summer. This plant is drought-tolerant and during dry spells can be seen, not only green but covered with flowers, on brown lawns and dry road-verges. A variable species in size and flower colour: several colour variants are favourite plants of the cottage garden.

J	F	M	A	M	J
J	A	S	O	N	D

Corn Marigold

Chrysanthemum segetum

ID FACT FILE

Height:
15–60 cm

Flowers:
Solitary heads, 35–65 mm across, disc and ray florets golden yellow

Leaves: Mostly oblong, deeply toothed, rather fleshy; the upper almost toothless, clasping the stem

Fruits: Heads of 1-seeded fruits, without hairs, the outer ones flattened

Lookalikes:
Ox-eye Daisy (p.211) has white ray florets.

Erect or ascending, often branched, hairless, bluish-green annual, of cultivated land, roadsides and waste places. Formerly it was a severe weed problem in arable fields, especially on more acid, sandy soils. It is widely distributed but decreasing in Britain and Ireland, although its use in commercial wild flower seed-mixtures may again expand its range somewhat. Corn Marigold was originally a native of the Mediterranean region that probably arrived here with ancient farmers.

J	F	M	A	M	J
J	A	S	O	N	D

Tansy

Tanacetum vulgare

ID FACT FILE

Height: 50–150 cm

Flowers: Heads 7–12 mm across, golden yellow, without ray florets, 10–70 in flat-topped clusters

Leaves: Fern-like, oblong, deeply lobed, toothed, dark green

Fruits: Heads of ribbed, 1-seeded fruits, without hairs

Lookalikes: Feverfew or Bachelor's Buttons (*Tanacetum parthenium*) is smaller, with yellowish-green leaves, and flowerheads with white ray florets; it rarely occurs far from houses.

Erect, leafy, sweetly aromatic perennial, forming clumps, the stems branched in the upper part; it is a plant of waste places, roadsides, hedgerows and riverbanks, often around houses or ruined buildings. It has long been used medicinally and is an ingredient of the Tansy puddings formerly eaten at Easter, and of drisheen, a spicy black pudding from SW Ireland. Like other aromatic members of the daisy and dandelion family, the fresh leaves discourage flies and other insects.

J	F	M	A	M	J
J	A	S	O	N	D

Ox-eye, or Moon, Daisy

Leucanthemum vulgare

ID FACT FILE

Height: 20–100 cm

Flowers: Heads 25–50 mm across, with yellow disc florets and white ray florets; bracts with brown or black margin

Leaves: Oval to spoon-shaped, toothed, dark green; upper ones oblong, clasping the stem

Fruits: Heads of 1-seeded fruits, without hairs

Lookalikes: A much larger plant than Daisy (p.199), which often occurs with it in grassland.

Erect, usually unbranched, short-lived perennial; a characteristic plant of old meadows, churchyards and coastal grassland and sand-dunes. A variable species: for example, dwarf plants occur on sea-cliffs and coastal heaths. In recent years it has become very common and conspicuous on newly landscaped motorway verges. Robust, branched plants with large leaves and flowers on road-verges derive from commercial wild flower seed, and are probably of garden origin.

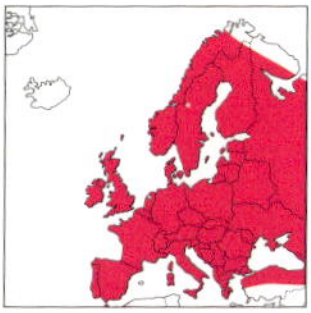

J	F	M	A	M	J
J	A	S	O	N	D

Mugwort

Artemisia vulgaris

ID FACT FILE

Height: 50–180 cm

Flowers: Tiny, in reddish-brown, egg-shaped heads, 2–3 cm across, without ray florets, grouped in loose clusters

Leaves: Much-lobed, the lobes spear-shaped or themselves deeply lobed, hairless above, white-hairy beneath

Fruits: Heads of nut-like, 1-seeded fruits, without hairs

Lookalikes: Wormwood (*Artemisia absinthium*) is aromatic, with silky-hairy, silvery leaves, and also occurs in waste places near houses or ruins.

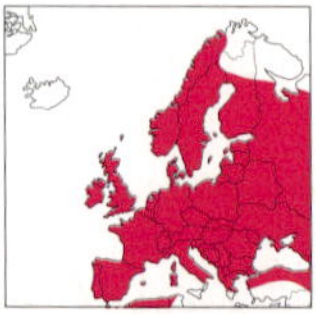

Tough, erect, untidy perennial of dry waysides, waste ground and derelict land, almost always near buildings or roads. In late summer this is the most typical plant flowering on dusty, urban and suburban roadsides, demolition sites, neglected pavements and waste ground. The dried leaves have served as a substitute for tobacco. Like St John's Wort (p.101), it was used to ward off evil spirits as part of the St John's Eve pagan festivities at the Summer Solstice.

J	F	M	A	M	J
J	A	S	O	N	D

Colt's-foot

Tussilago farfara

ID FACT FILE

Height: 10–30 cm

Flowers: Heads on stout, scaly stems, yellow; disc florets few, the ray florets orange beneath, in heads 20–35 mm across

Leaves: Appearing after flowers, all basal, heart-shaped, up to 25 cm across, toothed, cobweb-by beneath (also above at first)

Fruits: Heads of 1-seeded fruits, each with a 'parachute' of long hairs

Lookalikes: Dandelion (p.224) has ray florets only, and the flowers are produced on leafless stems at the same time as leaves.

Erect perennial, with thick, creeping rhizome, forming large patches on the bare ground of waste places, road-verges, banks of rivers and streams, and low sea-cliffs. Often found on clay soils, it is an early colonist of clay banks of rivers and at the seaside. It is one of the plants that occupies ground left bare by retreating Alpine glaciers. Colt's-foot has long held a reputation as a cure for coughs and illnesses of the chest. The flowers are one of the first indicators of spring.

J	F	M	A	M	J
J	A	S	O	N	D

Butterbur

Petasites hybridus

Erect perennial, with a creeping rhizome, forming large, conspicuous patches; rather local on the banks of streams and rivers, in damp woods and on road-verges. It prefers sandy or well-drained soils. The stout clusters of flowers are an impressive sight in early spring; later the immense leaves form great thickets. Most plants are male. The female plant, with flowerheads that elongate considerably in fruit, is very local in occurrence, mainly in parts of N England.

ID FACT FILE

Height: 10–30 cm, female plants elongating to 60 cm

Flowers: Pale lilac or yellowish, unscented, in large heads

Leaves: Appearing after flowers, all basal, rhubarb-like, up to 1 m across, toothed, cobwebby beneath (also above at first)

Fruits: Heads of 1-seeded fruits, each with a 'parachute' of hairs

Lookalikes: Winter Heliotrope (*Petasites fragrans*) has richly scented flowers in looser clusters, produced from November to March, with the leaves; it is a garden escape.

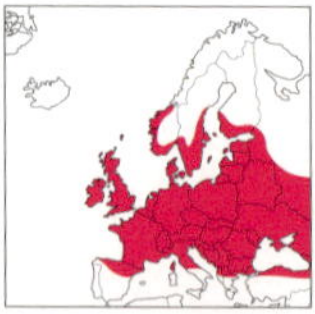

J	F	M	A	M	J
J	A	S	O	N	D

All through mild winters.

Groundsel

Senecio vulgaris

ID FACT FILE

Height: 5–40 cm

Flowers: Yellow, in shaving-brush-like heads 4–5 mm across, usually without ray florets, in loose clusters

Leaves: Coarsely and bluntly lobed and irregularly toothed

Fruits: Heads of 1-seeded fruits, each with 'parachute' of hairs

Lookalikes: Other species of groundsel or ragwort have conspicuous ray florets or sticky-hairy bracts.

Ubiquitous, erect, branched, rather hairy annual of waste places, walls, paths and pavements, cultivated ground, sand-dunes and shingle beaches. Groundsel is one of the first flowers of late winter and early spring, along with Chickweed (p.25), Shepherd's Purse (p.47) and Red Dead-nettle (p.154). Occasional plants with short ray florets may derive from crossing with Oxford Ragwort (p.217). The first half of the scientific name refers to the white fruiting heads (Latin: *senex*, old man).

J	F	M	A	M	J
J	A	S	O	N	D

Ragwort

Senecio jacobaea

ID FACT FILE

Height: 30–150 cm

Flowers: Bright yellow, in heads 15–25 mm across, with ray florets present, in often dense, flat-topped clusters

Leaves: Lyre-shaped or deeply lobed, irregularly toothed, usually hairy beneath; upper leaves clasping the stem

Fruits: Heads of 1-seeded fruits, each with a 'parachute' of hairs

Lookalikes: Oxford Ragwort (p.217) has lobed, less complexly dissected, toothed leaves, and laxer clusters of flower-heads.

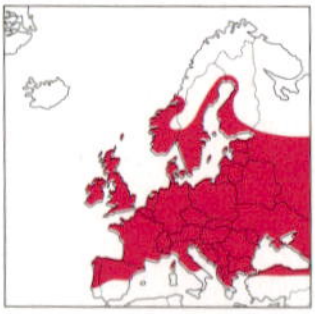

An erect, leafy biennial or short-lived perennial of waysides, waste ground, pastures, sand-dunes and shingle beaches. The leaves give off an unpleasant smell when bruised, hence local names such as 'Stinking Willie'. It is a poisonous plant that can be a great menace to livestock, especially horses. The caterpillars of the Cinnabar Moth feed on Ragwort, accumulating its poisonous chemicals to protect themselves against birds, hence their yellow- and black-striped warning colours.

J	F	M	A	M	J
J	A	S	O	N	D

Oxford Ragwort

Senecio squalidus

ID FACT FILE

Height: 20–60 cm

Flowers: Bright yellow, in heads 15–25 mm across, with ray florets, in loose, flat-topped clusters

Leaves: Deeply, coarsely and bluntly lobed, and irregularly toothed

Fruits: Heads of 1-seeded fruits, each with a 'parachute' of hairs

Lookalikes: Ragwort (p.216) has more complexly dissected, toothed leaves and denser, flat-topped clusters of flowerheads.

Erect or ascending, branched annual, biennial or perennial of walls, derelict buildings, waste ground, paths and road-verges, especially on railway ballast. It is scattered throughout Britain; in Ireland it occurs mostly in Belfast, Cork and Dublin. Introduced from the mountains of S Europe, the plant escaped on to walls in Oxford from the Botanic Garden during the 19th century, thence along the railway network to other regions. Today it is still spreading and even occurs as a garden weed.

J	F	M	A	M	J
J	A	S	O	N	D

Lesser Burdock

Arctium minus

ID FACT FILE

Height: 50–150 cm

Flowers: Purple, in spherical heads, 15–20 mm across, in long, loose clusters; bracts dense, hooked

Leaves: Heart-shaped, up to 50 cm long, cottony beneath, with long, hollow stalks; upper leaves smaller, narrower

Fruits: Egg-shaped 'bur' heads 20–35 mm across, enclosed by involucre of stiff, hooked hairs; each head is dispersed as a unit

Lookalikes: Great Burdock (*Arctium lappa*), has fewer flowerheads, 30–45 mm across.

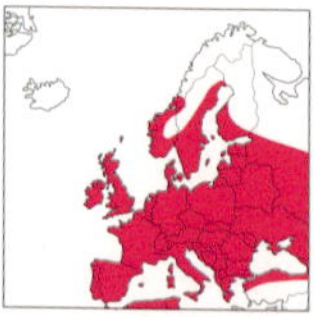

A robust, leafy, downy biennial, with many, branched stems, common in dry woods, on roadsides and in waste places. The hooked burs adhere readily to clothing or fur, dispersing the seeds. At an annual fair in August, the Burry Man, his costume densely studded with these burs, parades in strict silence around South Queensferry, West Lothian. The plant is such a feature of woods and waysides that it sometimes appeared as a detail in the paintings and sketches of John Constable.

Common, or Spear, Thistle

Cirsium vulgare

J	F	M	A	M	J
J	A	S	O	N	D

ID FACT FILE

Height: 30–180 cm

Flowers: Purple, scented, in egg-shaped heads 3–5 cm across, 1–3 in branched clusters; bracts spine-tipped

Leaves: Spear-shaped, deeply lobed, with coarse, irregular lobes, each with a spine

Fruits: Heads of 1-seeded fruits, each with a 'parachute' of soft, feathery hairs (thistle-down)

Lookalikes: Creeping Thistle (*Cirsium arvense*) is a perennial forming great patches; flower-heads, mauve, 15–20 mm across, with purple bracts, in loose clusters.

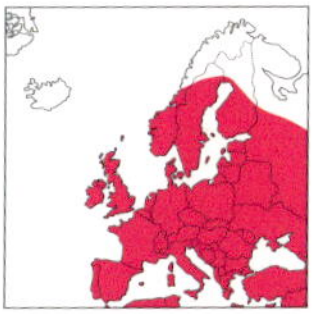

Erect, leafy, ferociously spiny, hairy annual or biennial of pastures, roadsides and waste ground. This is probably the true Scots Thistle; the larger thistle of that name is a rare plant in Scotland. It is said that thistles impeded a surprise night attack by the Danes during the Battle of Largs by pricking the attackers, whose consequent cries of pain alerted the defenders. Like those of other thistles, the flowers are attractive to bumblebees. The fruits are often eaten by beetle larvae.

J	F	M	A	M	J
J	A	S	O	N	D

Marsh Thistle

Cirsium palustre

Erect, little-branched, hairy, dark green or purplish biennial, with (usually) a single, winged, spiny stem; widespread in marshes, damp woods and grassy places, and on western sea-cliffs. The huge cartwheels of the leaf-rosettes and the tall flowering stems are a characteristic feature of damp grassland, especially where the plant is commonest: on more acid soils in the north and west of Britain and in Ireland. The flowers attract numbers of bumblebees and other insects.

ID FACT FILE

Height: 50–180 cm

Flowers: Purple or white, in egg-shaped heads, 15–20 mm across, in crowded, leafy clusters; bracts weakly spine-tipped

Leaves: Rather narrow, spear-shaped, deeply lobed, with densely spiny margins

Fruits: Heads of 1-seeded fruits, each with a parachute of soft, feathery hairs

Lookalikes: Creeping Thistle (*Cirsium arvense*), a perennial that forms great patches, has heads of mauve flowers in flatter clusters.

J	F	M	A	M	J
J	A	S	O	N	D

Greater Knapweed

Centaurea scabiosa

ID FACT FILE

Height: 50–180 cm

Flowers: Reddish-purple, in heads 3–5 cm across; outer ray florets long; bracts green, with brown, toothed margin

Leaves: Oblong or spear-shaped, deeply lobed

Fruits: Heads of 1-seeded fruits, each with a crown of bristly hairs, enclosed by bracts

Lookalikes: Common Knapweed (p.222) sometimes has long, stalked ray florets; Cornflower (*Centaurea cyanus*) is a slender annual with blue flowers; once a cornfield weed, now mostly a garden escape.

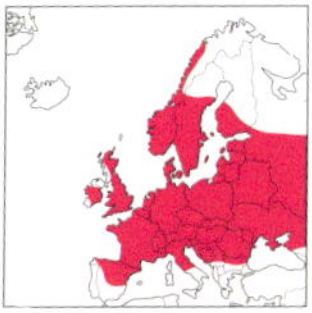

Handsome, erect, branched, hairy perennial of dry grassland, hedge-banks, road verges, sand-dunes and sea-cliffs, especially on lime-rich soils. Seen even from a speeding car or train, this conspicuous plant is a good indicator of whether the soil is over chalk and limestone. It is widespread in England, but local in Scotland and much of Wales and Ireland. Knapweeds are a large and variable group of species in Europe – more than 220 are known. Only two are widespread in Britain and Ireland.

J	F	M	A	M	J
J	A	S	O	N	D

Hardheads or Common Knapweed

Centaurea nigra

ID FACT FILE

Height: 30–180 cm

Flowers: Reddish- or pinkish-purple, in heads 2–4 cm across; outer ray florets rarely long; bracts brown, fringed

Leaves: Oval or spear-shaped, the upper ones narrower

Fruits: Heads of 1-seeded fruits, with crown of short, bristly hairs, enclosed by bracts

Lookalikes: Greater Knapweed (p.221) has compound leaves and flowerheads 3–5 cm across, always with stalked ray florets.

Tough-stemmed, erect, branched, downy perennial, a widespread and common plant of grasslands, waysides and sea-cliffs. Nevertheless, like so many of our wild flowers, it is not as common as it was formerly over much of England; plants from the few surviving old lowland meadows tend to flower earlier and frequently have long, stalked ray florets similar to those of Greater Knapweed (p.221). The hard, knobbly flowerheads give the plant its apt popular name.

J	F	M	A	M	J
J	A	S	O	N	D

Chicory

Cichorium intybus

ID FACT FILE

Height: 30–120 cm

Flowers: Pale blue, in heads 3–5 cm across, 1–3 in axils of upper leaves

Leaves: Basal leaves in a rosette, deeply and coarsely lobed; upper leaves spear-shaped, pointed

Fruits: Heads of nut-like, 1-seeded fruits, without hairs

Lookalikes: Blue Sowthistle (*Cicerbita macrophylla*) is erect, up to 2 m tall, the flowers in branched, flat-topped clusters; introduced, mainly on roadsides.

Erect or spreading, untidy perennial, with stiffly branched, zigzag, grooved stems, of waste places, dry waysides and field margins. It is commonest on lime-rich soils. The flowers look their best in the morning, fading after midday. Chicory is widely cultivated, especially in gardens, where it has long been a valued winter salad. It also has medicinal (mainly diuretic and laxative) properties, and the roasted roots are used as a substitute for coffee, especially in C Europe.

J	F	M	A	M	J
J	A	S	O	N	D

All through mild winters.

ID FACT FILE

Height: 5–40 cm

Flowers: Yellow, 25–40 mm across, solitary on long, hollow stems, the outer ray florets often greenish, brownish or reddish beneath

Leaves: In a basal rosette, deeply lobed or toothed

Fruits: Heads of 1-seeded fruits, each with a 'parachute' of feathery hairs

Lookalikes: The smooth, hollow stems, large, solitary flowers, and down-turned bracts, distinguish this variable species.

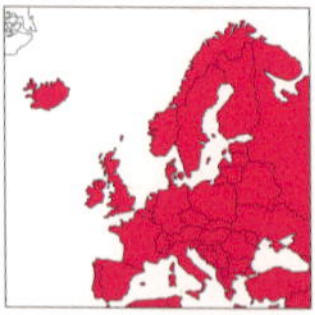

Dandelion

Taraxacum officinale

Familiar, tufted, very sparsely hairy perennial, of grasslands, road-verges, sand-dunes, wet places, open and disturbed ground, notably as a garden weed of lawns and flower-beds. In recent years, being slightly salt-tolerant, it has spread along road-verges on a massive scale; in April it can be a magnificent sight. The root makes an agreeable substitute for coffee, and dandelion latex provided the former Soviet Union with rubber during World War II. A very variable plant that botanists divide into hundreds of similar 'microspecies'.

J	F	M	A	M	J
J	A	S	O	N	D

Common Cat's-ear

Hypochoeris radicata

ID FACT FILE

Height: 10–60 cm

Flowers: Yellow, 25–40 mm across, solitary, erect in bud, the outer ray florets greenish or greyish beneath

Leaves: In a basal rosette, deeply lobed or toothed

Fruits: Heads of 1-seeded fruits, each with a 'parachute' of feathery hairs

Lookalikes: Lesser Hawkbit (*Leontodon taraxacoides*) has unbranched stems and flowerheads 12–20 mm across, nodding in bud.

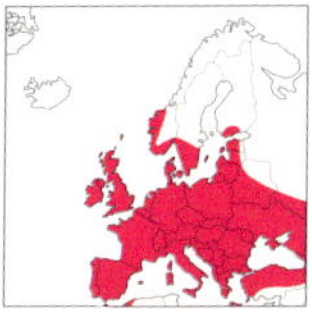

Erect, tufted, usually branched perennial of grassland, especially waysides, sand-dunes and lawns. It flourishes on a range of soils but requires good drainage. This is the commonest of several yellow, dandelion-like flowers so hard to distinguish from one another, and the one most likely to be seen on garden lawns or in parks, where it forms prominent green patches in dry spells. The common name of this plant derives, rather obscurely, from the shape of the tiny bracts on the flowering stems. The hairless, leafless, branched stems are distinctive.

J	F	M	A	M	J
J	A	S	O	N	D

Autumn Hawkbit

Leontodon autumnalis

ID FACT FILE

HEIGHT: 10–60 cm

FLOWERS: Yellow, 12–35 mm across, solitary, erect in bud, the outer florets often reddish-streaked beneath

LEAVES: All in a basal rosette, very deeply lobed, shiny

FRUITS: Heads of 1-seeded fruits, each with a 'parachute' of feathery hairs

LOOKALIKES: Lesser Hawkbit (*Leontodon taraxacoides*), of more lime-rich soils, has shallowly lobed leaves and flowerheads 12–20 mm across, nodding in bud, the outer florets greyish-violet beneath.

Erect, somewhat branched, sparsely hairy perennial, widespread and frequently abundant in dry and damp grassland, waysides and open stony ground such as lake-shores, especially on more acid soils. This is the most conspicuous of the yellow dandelion-like wild flowers that appear in late summer and early autumn. The hawkbits and their relatives are very difficult to tell apart, requiring careful examination of leaf-hairs, and other small features, with a lens.

J	F	M	A	M	J
J	A	S	O	N	D

Bristly Oxtongue

Picris echioides

ID FACT FILE

Height: 30–100 cm

Flowers: Rather pale yellow, 20–25 mm across, in branched clusters; 5 outer bracts large, triangular

Leaves: Oblong, untoothed or toothed, prickly, with swollen-based bristles; upper leaves smaller, heart-shaped, clasping the stem

Fruits: Large, conspicuous heads of 1-seeded fruits, each with a 'parachute' of feathery hairs

Lookalikes: Hawkweed Oxtongue (*Picris hieracioides*) has spear-shaped lower leaves and narrow bracts; rare in Ireland.

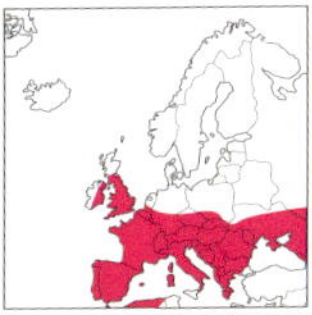

Untidy, ascending or weakly erect, bristly annual, biennial or short-lived perennial, with rather stiff, branched stems; locally frequent in rough grassland and disturbed ground such as field margins and road-verges, northwards to Yorkshire and near the coasts of S and E Ireland. It prefers lime-rich, clayey soils. Two different types of fruit are produced: 3–5 fruits at the margin of each head are larger, with a smaller parachute of hairs, and are shed close to the parent plant.

J	F	M	A	M	J
J	A	S	O	N	D

Goat's-beard

Tragopogon pratensis

ID FACT FILE

Height: 30–70 cm

Flowers: Yellow, in solitary, long-stalked heads, 3–5 cm across; bracts 8, up to 3 cm long, pointed

Leaves: Grass-like, rather greyish-green and fleshy, pointed, closely sheathing the stem

Fruits: Conspicuous heads of 1-seeded fruits, each with a large 'parachute' of stiff, feathery hairs

Lookalikes: This plant has an unmistakable combination of grass-like leaves and yellow, dandelion-like flowers.

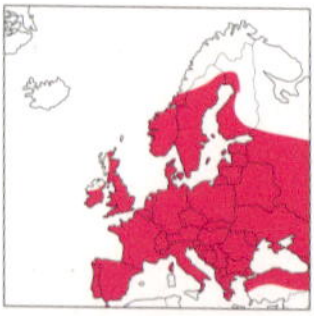

Erect, annual, biennial or short-lived perennial, arising from a narrow, parsnip-like root, of dry grassland, road-verges and waste places. The flowers close after midday, giving the plant its local name of 'Jack- (or John-)-go-to-bed-at-noon'. The closely related, similar but purple-flowered Salsify (*Tragopogon porrifolius*) is sometimes grown as a root vegetable. The large fruits demonstrate clearly the features of the 'dandelion-type' seed-fruit unit and dispersal mechanism.

J	F	M	A	M	J
J	A	S	O	N	D

Corn, or Perennial, Sow-thistle

Sonchus arvensis

ID FACT FILE

Height: 50–150 cm

Flowers: Golden yellow, in heads 3–5 cm across, in loose clusters; bracts and flower-stems with yellowish hairs, very rarely hairless

Leaves: Oblong to spear-shaped, deeply lobed, spiny-toothed; upper leaves clasping stem

Fruits: Heads of 1-seeded fruits, each with a 'parachute' of hairs

Lookalikes: Smooth Sow-thistle (p.230) and Prickly Sow-thistle (*Sonchus asper*) are annual, with paler flowerheads 20–25 mm across.

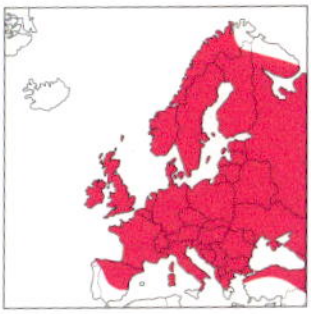

Erect, leafy perennial, with a network of far-creeping rhizomes and more slender roots; forming sometimes quite extensive patches on cultivated land, field margins, banks of streams and rivers, sand-dunes and shingle beaches. Even quite small fragments of root are able to grow into new plants, making this a noxious weed if it is not controlled. This is one of the handsomest and most conspicuous wild flowers of the late summer and early autumn countryside.

J	F	M	A	M	J
J	A	S	O	N	D

Smooth Sow-thistle

Sonchus oleraceus

ID FACT FILE

Height: 30–120 cm

Flowers: Rather pale yellow, the ray florets purplish beneath, in numerous heads 20–25 mm across; bracts mostly hairless

Leaves: Variable in shape, deeply lobed, with a large terminal lobe, spiny-toothed; upper leaves clasping stem

Fruits: Heads of 1-seeded fruits, each with a 'parachute' of hairs

Lookalikes: Prickly Sow-thistle (*Sonchus asper*) is often taller and less branched, with more clustered flower-heads, prickly leaves and sticky-hairy bracts.

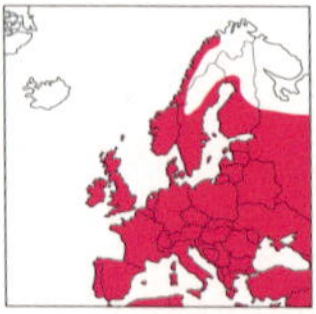

Erect, branched, often reddish-tinged annual; occurs mostly on cultivated ground where it can be a troublesome weed, although it will grow almost anywhere, even on the tops of walls or in the crevices of tarmac. The French feed this plant to edible snails, whilst in Greece and elsewhere it is eaten as a winter salad, as it was once (like many dandelion relatives) in England. The first half of the scientific name derives from *Sonchos*, the ancient Greek name for this plant.

J	F	M	A	M	J
J	A	S	O	N	D

Nipplewort

Lapsana communis

ID FACT FILE

Height: 30–120 cm

Flowers: Pale yellow, in numerous heads 15–20 mm across, in loose, branched clusters

Leaves: Oval, deeply lobed with large terminal lobe, toothed; upper stalkless, spear-shaped, untoothed

Fruits: Narrowly egg-shaped heads of nut-like, 1-seeded fruits, without hairs, partly enclosed by the bracts

Lookalikes: The fruits, without hairs, are unique among yellow dandelion-like flowers.

Erect, branched, leafy annual or biennial, hairy in lower part: a common plant of waysides, hedgerows, wood margins, shady gardens and cultivated land. It can sometimes be a troublesome weed. It grows best on heavier clay soils. The young leaves were once used as a salad, and slightly larger, more long-lived plants are found here and there, which may be relics of former cultivation. The common name derives less from any healing properties than from a reference to the shape of the buds.

J	F	M	A	M	J
J	A	S	O	N	D

Mouse-ear Hawkweed

Pilosella vulgaris

ID FACT FILE

Height: 5–20 cm, sometimes up to 35 cm

Flowers: Pale yellow, the florets usually red-striped beneath, 18–25 mm across, solitary, on long, leafless stems

Leaves: Basal ones in a rosette, oblong to spear-shaped, blunt, with long, white hairs above, white-downy beneath

Fruits: Heads of 1-seeded fruits, each with a 'parachute' of hairs

Lookalikes: Fox-and-Cubs or Grim-the-Collier (*Pilosella aurantiacum*), with blackish hairs and clustered orange flowerheads, is a garden escape.

Hairy perennial, with erect flowering stems and extensively creeping, leafy runners, forming often large patches in open ground or short turf of dry pastures, heaths, rocky ground, banks, walls and lawns. It is a characteristic plant of dry road and railway cuttings, banks on old lawns, and earth-filled stone walls, especially on sandy soils or near the sea. The hawkweeds are divided by botanists into many 'microspecies', but this plant is easily recognised by the pale yellow flowers and long runners.

J	F	M	A	M	J
J	A	S	O	N	D

Common Water-plantain

Alisma plantago-aquatica

ID FACT FILE

Height: 30–100 cm

Flowers: White or pale lilac, up to 10 cm across, in loose, long-stalked, domed clusters; 3 petals and sepals

Leaves: All basal in a rosette, oval to spear-shaped, rounded or heart-shaped at base

Fruits: Flattish head of 1-seeded fruits in a ring

Lookalikes: Arrowhead (*Sagittaria sagittifolia*) has arrow-shaped leaves, larger flowers and fruits in a spherical cluster; it occurs in ponds, canals and slow-moving rivers.

Erect, hairless, aquatic perennial of lakes, marshes, canals and ponds; it survives even in the muddiest, scruffiest ponds and streams. It is widespread in Britain and Ireland, although rare in N Scotland. Individual flowers open after midday and usually wither within 24 hours. This is the commonest of five native water-plantains, which resemble the buttercups and water-buttercups (pp.33–41), having similar flowers (but only three, not five, petals), many stamens and one-seeded fruits.

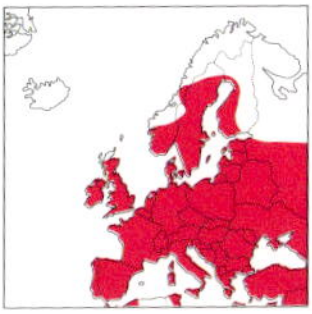

J	F	M	A	M	J
J	A	S	O	N	D

Flowering Rush

Butomus umbellatus

A striking, erect, hairless, aquatic perennial, with a creeping rhizome, of slow streams and rivers, reed-beds and ditches; widespread though local in England, but rare in Wales (except Anglesey), Scotland and most of Ireland. This is one of our handsomest aquatic plants, which can add grandeur to the shabbiest canal bank; hence the local name of 'Pride-of-the-Thames', commemorating the river where John Gerard, author of the famous 1597 *Herball*, knew it in the 16th century.

ID FACT FILE

Height: 50–150 cm

Flowers: Pink with darker veins, 25–30 mm across, many, in a domed cluster or umbel; 6 perianth-segments; carpels 6, stamens 9, both red

Leaves: All basal, 3-angled, narrow, rush-like

Fruits: Head of purple capsules, united in a ring

Lookalikes: Common Water-plantain (p.233) and Arrowhead (*Sagittaria sagittifolia*, p.233, Lookalikes) have smaller, white flowers and broader leaves.

J	F	M	A	M	J
J	A	S	O	N	D

Bog Asphodel

Narthecium ossifragum

ID FACT FILE

Height: 15–45 cm

Flowers: 6–10 mm across, bright yellow, the perianth-segments green beneath, 6–20 in a stiff spike; stamens orange

Leaves: In 2 ranks, sword-shaped, pointed; the upper scale-like

Fruits: Narrowly egg-shaped, tapered, pointed capsules, splitting into 3 segments

Lookalikes: This distinctive plant of bogs is unlikely to be confused with any other.

A rhizomatous, erect, hairless perennial of bogs, wet heaths and moors. It is very common over much of the west and north of the British Isles but is rare in S and E England. The flowers and flowering stems become dark orange after flowering, becoming a feature of boglands. It was formerly a source of dye whose uses included – like henna – colouring women's hair. The plant is poisonous to sheep. True asphodels, with yellow or white flowers, occur in S Europe and the Mediterranean region.

J	F	M	A	M	J
J	A	S	O	N	D

Fritillary or Snake's Head

Fritillaria meleagris

ID FACT FILE

Height: 20–40 cm

Flowers: Solitary, sometimes in pairs, bell-shaped, nodding, 30–45 mm long, dull purple mottled with purplish-brown, or white

Leaves: 3–6, all on the stem, narrowly strap-like, pointed, greyish-green

Fruits: Rather squat, oblong capsules, splitting into 3 segments

Lookalikes: No similar wild flower occurs in N Europe, although other species of fritillary are seen in gardens.

An elegant, erect, hairless perennial, arising from a bulb, in damp meadows of S and C England, especially old water-meadows of the Thames Valley. Fritillary has declined severely during this century, as a result of the draining, ploughing and fertilising of meadowland. However, at some surviving sites – several of them nature reserves – it often occurs in crowds of thousands. Three flower colours – purple, white with pink veins, and white with green veins – represent natural genetic variation.

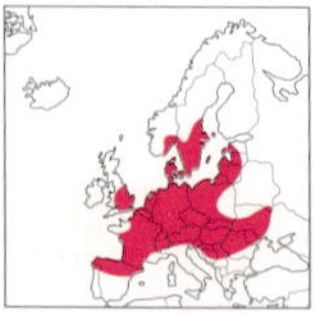

J	F	M	A	M	J
J	A	S	O	N	D

Bluebell or Wild Hyacinth

Hyacinthoides non-scripta

ID FACT FILE

Height: 20–40 cm

Flowers: Violet-blue, very rarely white, bell-shaped, nodding, 15–20 mm long, richly scented, in a drooping, 1-sided cluster

Leaves: Many, all basal, strap-like, folded in a V, pointed, about as long as the flowering stems

Fruits: Almost spherical, 3-angled capsules; seeds black, shiny

Lookalikes: Spanish Bluebell (*Hyacinthoides hispanicus*), more robust and with paler blue, lilac or white flowers, is a garden escape.

Erect, hairless perennial, arising from a bulb and sometimes growing in vast crowds; widespread in woods, scrub, heaths and hedgerows. In western Britain, parts of Ireland and in Scotland it grows on sea-cliffs. In Scotland it is usually known as Wild Hyacinth; Harebell (p.195) is the Bluebell of Scotland. This familiar and much-loved plant is restricted to far W Europe, and the magnificent bluebell woods of Britain and Ireland represent its world stronghold. There is no floral display like them.

J	F	M	A	M	J
J	A	S	O	N	D

Ramsons

Allium ursinum

ID FACT FILE

Height: 20–50 cm

Flowers: White, bell-shaped, nodding, 8–12 mm long, 6–20, in a loose, domed cluster or umbel

Leaves: All basal, elliptical, bright green, hairless

Fruits: Deeply 3-lobed capsules

Lookalikes: Crow Garlic (*Allium vineale*) is a plant of dry grassland and fields, with narrow, tubular leaves and dense, spherical heads of greenish or purplish flowers intermixed with small bulbs.

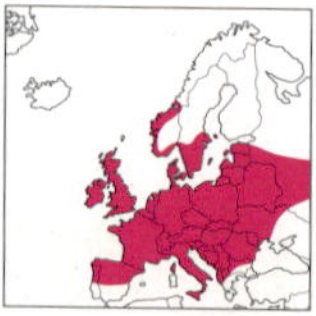

Erect, hairless perennial, arising from a bulb, of damp woods, hedge-banks and shady streamsides. The plant smells strongly of garlic when bruised. It is a characteristic plant of ancient woodlands. The leaves are edible and are said to add zest to peanut butter sandwiches! However, on a spring day they can make a woodland walk a very smelly experience. This distinctive plant is related to the wild onions and leeks, which are narrow-leaved plants mostly of open, rocky or sandy ground. It is sometimes grown in cottage gardens.

J	F	M	A	M	J
J	A	S	O	N	D

Wild Daffodil

Narcissus pseudonarcissus

ID FACT FILE

Height: 15–40 cm

Flowers: Yellow, nodding, slightly scented, 35–60 mm across, the central trumpet deeper in colour; buds enclosed by papery sheath

Leaves: All basal, narrow, strap-shaped, greyish-green

Fruits: Egg-shaped capsules 10–25 mm long

Lookalikes: Escaped garden daffodils, often planted in woods and on banks, are more robust, with larger, uniformly yellow flowers.

An erect, hairless perennial, arising from a fleshy bulb, forming clumps, extensive patches and colonies; local in grassland, open woods, coppices, pastures and churchyards, on slightly damp but well-drained, humus-rich soils. Scattered throughout England, but commonest in the west, and parts of Wales; introduced in Scotland and Ireland. The flowers locally colour the early spring landscape. The whole plant is poisonous and is avoided by grazing animals.

J	F	M	A	M	J
J	A	S	O	N	D

Snowdrop

Galanthus nivalis

ID FACT FILE

Height: 10–25 cm

Flowers: Solitary, nodding, white, scented, the inner 3 perianth-segments notched, with a green patch near edge

Leaves: All basal, narrow, strap-shaped, greyish-green, blunt

Fruits: Egg-shaped capsules 8–15 mm long, on long, nodding stalks

Lookalikes: Summer Snowflake *(Leucojum aestivum)*, up to 60cm tall, with wider, green leaves and 3–5 flowers in a cluster, occurs in wet woods of the Thames Valley and elsewhere.

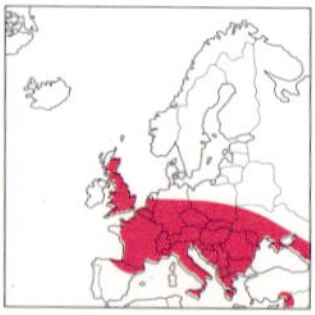

An erect, hairless perennial, arising from small bulbs to form clumps and patches; often abundant and brightening woods, hedges, streamsides and churchyards in late winter. It is perhaps native in a few areas of SW England, such as the Mendip Hills, but most evidence suggests that it is an ancient introduction frequently associated with both pagan and Christian sites. It is the symbolic flower of the feast of Candlemas (2 February), commemorating the purification of the Virgin Mary.

J	F	M	A	M	J
J	A	S	O	N	D

Yellow Flag

Iris pseudacorus

ID FACT FILE

Height: 50–150 cm

Flowers: 8–10 cm across, yellow, 4–12 in a cluster, usually 1–3 open at once, each with a sheathing bract; sepals broad, nodding

Leaves: Evergreen, narrow, spear-shaped, sharp-edged, pointed

Fruits: Cylindrical capsules 4–8 cm long, splitting into 3 segments; seeds brown

Lookalikes: Stinking Iris (*Iris foetidissima*), with violet or sometimes pale yellow flowers, narrower leaves and scarlet seeds, is a plant of woods, hedges and sand-dunes, mainly in S England.

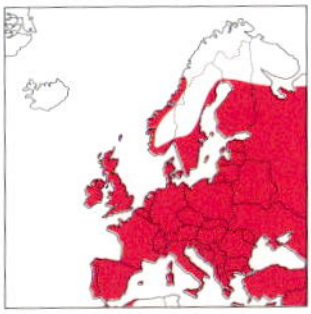

Erect perennial with stout rhizomes and robust flowering stems, common in marshes, ditches and on the shores of rivers, canals, lakes, ponds and flooded gravel-pits; widespread and frequently abundant throughout Britain and Ireland. The rhizome yields a black dye. One of our stateliest and most distinctive wild flowers, this handsome plant has survived despite the destruction of so many wetland habitats. The flowers are much visited by bumblebees. The seeds float and are dispersed by water.

J	F	M	A	M	J
J	A	S	O	N	D

Black Bryony

Tamus communis

ID FACT FILE

Height: 1–4 m

Flowers: Greenish-yellow, 3–6 mm across, male and female in separate clusters; perianth-segments 6

Leaves: Up to 15 cm long, stalked, heart-shaped, pointed, shiny

Fruits: Loose clusters of very distinctive, spherical scarlet berries

Lookalikes: White Bryony (p.106), which has ivy-like leaves and tendrils, is not related.

Hairless, climbing, clockwise-twining perennial, with a branched, blackish tuber, of woods, scrub and hedgerows. It is commonest in S England, becoming less frequent northwards and reaching its N European limit in N England; in Ireland it occurs only around Lough Gill in Co. Sligo. The young shoots were formerly eaten like asparagus and are still to be seen on sale in S Europe. The attractive berries are poisonous. This is one of just four European representatives of an important tropical plant family.

J	F	M	A	M	J
J	A	S	O	N	D

Lords-and-ladies or Cuckoo-pint

Arum maculatum

ID FACT FILE

HEIGHT: 20–30 cm

FLOWERS: Club-shaped cluster within a solitary, conspicuous, pale green, sometimes purplish, envelope or spathe up to 25 cm long

LEAVES: All basal, long-stalked, arrow-shaped, shiny, sometimes purple-spotted

FRUITS: Cylindrical heads, 4–8 cm long, of scarlet berries

LOOKALIKES: There are several less common species related to Lords-and-ladies, most of them garden escapes.

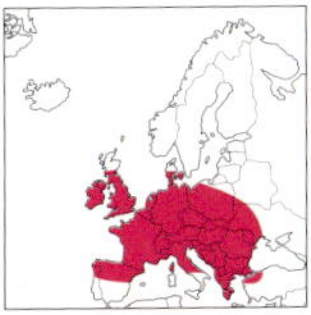

Erect, hairless perennial, with a tuberous rhizome, forming clumps in woods, hedges and shady places, sometimes in gardens, as far north as Fife. The curious flowers, enclosed in the cowl-like spathe, have attracted many local names, often rude or derogatory towards the clergy ('Jack-in-the-pulpit'), but including the wonderful 'Kitty-come-down-the-lane-jump-up-and-kiss-me'! Starch from the tubers was used like arrowroot and to starch laundry, not least the elaborate ruffs of Elizabethan England. Few wild flowers are so distinctive.

J	F	M	A	M	J
J	A	S	O	N	D

Duckweed

Lemna minor

ID FACT FILE

Height: Fronds 1.5–5 mm across

Flowers: Minute, enclosed in a sheath; stamens 1, ovules 2

Leaves: Green shoots reduced to a flat, 3-veined frond

Fruits: Minute, rarely formed

Lookalikes: Common Duckweed is by far the commonest of the 6 species of duckweed that occur in Britain and Ireland.

Tiny, floating, aquatic plant, each frond with a single root, forming a green mat on the surface of the water; common in still waters of lakes, ponds and streams, garden pools, permanent puddles and ruts of tracks. It is much eaten by wildfowl, hence the name. The plant rarely flowers. A very similar plant, Least Duckweed (*Lemna minuta*), with tiny, 1-veined fronds, was first recorded in Britain only in 1977 but is spreading rapidly in rivers and canals, where it forms green bands by banks and in eddies.

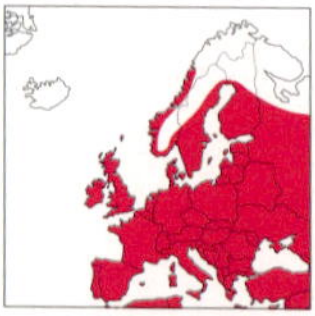

J	F	M	A	M	J
J	A	S	O	N	D

Branched Bur-reed

Sparganium erectum

ID FACT FILE

Height: 30–150 cm

Flowers: Small, grouped in male and female, spherical heads on 3–8 branches; male clusters above, smaller, yellow

Leaves: Narrow, strap-shaped, stiff; sometimes floating

Fruits: Bur-like spherical clusters

Lookalikes: Unbranched Bur-reed (*Sparganium emersum*), less common, has more or less unbranched stems; it has erect or floating leaves.

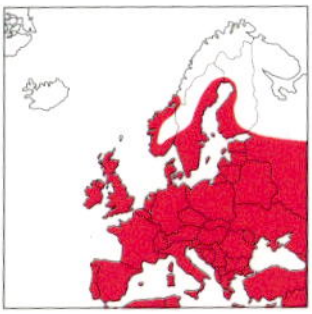

Robust, rhizomatous, erect, hairless perennial, of marshes and shallow water and exposed mud in ditches, ponds and disused canals; occurs throughout Britain and Ireland, although local in many districts. There are three other native bur-reeds, usually with floating leaves in deeper water, all of which have the similar distinctive flowerheads; only two are at all widespread, the two rarer species being found mostly in peaty pools and lakes in W Scotland and W Ireland.

J	F	M	A	M	J
J	A	S	O	N	D

Bulrush or Reedmace

Typha latifolia

ID FACT FILE

Height: 1–3 m

Flowers: Tiny, the female ones in cylindrical, sausage-like spikes 8–15 cm long; the male ones immediately above

Leaves: Strap-shaped, 8–20 mm wide

Fruits: Tiny, clustered in the dark brown, cylindrical spikes; seeds packed amongst soft, brownish hairs

Lookalikes: Lesser Bulrush or Reedmace (*Typha angustifolia*) has leaves c.4 mm wide and male and female flower-clusters slightly separated.

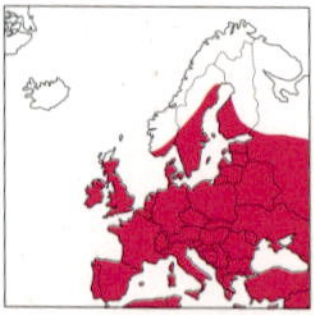

Robust, reed-like, aquatic perennial with creeping rhizome; forming dense stands in reed-swamps, lakes, ponds and slow-flowing streams and rivers. The spikes of fruit explode when ripe and dry, releasing huge numbers of seeds and the hairs (which represent reduced perianth-segments) that pack them within the 'mace'. This is the true Bulrush, as depicted in Victorian illustrations of the infant Moses, although botanists often apply this name to the Common Club-rush, which is related to the sedges.

J	F	M	A	M	J
J	A	S	O	N	D

Early Purple Orchid

Orchis mascula

ID FACT FILE

Height: 10–40 cm

Flowers: Purple, sometimes pink or white, with a 3-lobed lip, 6–8 mm long, smelling somewhat of cats, in dense cylindrical spikes

Leaves: Oblong, purple-spotted, the upper ones narrow

Fruits: Twisted, cylindrical capsules containing dust-like seeds

Lookalikes: Common and Heath Spotted-orchid (p.248) have paler flowers in a denser spike and flower a few weeks later.

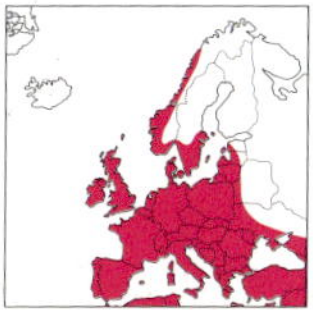

An erect perennial, arising from two egg-shaped tubers, of woods, hedge-banks, pastures and low cliffs by the sea. It is somewhat local, but in the north and west, for example Cornwall and the Burren of Co. Clare, it is commoner than Common Spotted-orchid (p.248), which it also replaces on clay soils. It often grows with Bluebells (p.237). This earliest-flowering of our native orchids is famous in literature as the 'long purples' of drowned Ophelia's garland in Shakespeare's *Hamlet*.

J	F	M	A	M	J
J	A	S	O	N	D

Common Spotted-orchid

Dactylorhiza fuchsii

ID FACT FILE

Height: 15–60 cm

Flowers: Pink, lilac or pinkish-purple, rarely white, with a deeply 3-lobed lip, 6–10 mm long, in dense, conical spike

Leaves: Spear-shaped or oblong, dark-spotted, the upper ones narrow

Fruits: Twisted, cylindrical capsules containing dust-like seeds

Lookalikes: Heath Spotted-orchid (*Dactylorhiza maculata*) has flowers with a shallowly lobed lip and grows on acid soils. Early Purple Orchid (p.247) has purple flowers in a loose spike a few weeks earlier.

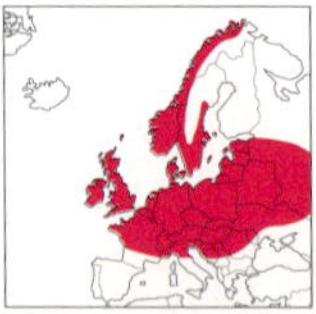

An erect, short-lived perennial, arising from a tuber divided into fat, finger-like lobes; sometimes frequent in open woods, scrub, dry or damp grassland, road and railway embankments, marshes, sand-dunes and even untended lawns. This is the commonest native orchid, still to be seen in great crowds, even on urban waste ground, over most of Britain and Ireland. It is a variable species that crosses with other related orchids: a distinctive variant with white flowers is found in the Burren of Co. Clare.

J	F	M	A	M	J
J	A	S	O	N	D

Pyramidal Orchid

Anacamptis pyramidalis

ID FACT FILE

Height: 15–40 cm

Flowers: Crimson- or purplish-red, rarely white, slightly fragrant, with a wedge-shaped, deeply 3-lobed lip 6–8 mm long, in dense pyramidal spike; spur slender, up to 14 mm long

Leaves: Oblong or spear-shaped, pointed, the upper ones narrow

Fruits: Twisted, cylindrical capsules containing dust-like seeds

Lookalikes: Common Spotted-orchid (p.248) has spotted leaves, and paler flowers in a more cylindrical spike.

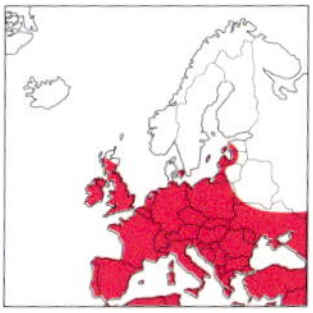

Erect perennial, the leafy stem arising from two almost spherical tubers, a local but sometimes quite common plant of scrub, grassland, dry banks and sand-dunes northwards to Fife and the Hebrides. In the sand-dune grassland or machair of W Ireland and, more locally, in W Scotland, it is a characteristic plant of hay-meadows. Plants in Ireland often have more richly and intensely coloured flowers. Pollination is by long-tongued butterflies and moths which seek the nectar in the long spur.

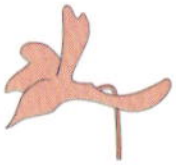

J	F	M	A	M	J
J	A	S	O	N	D

Bee Orchid

Ophrys apifera

ID FACT FILE

Height: 10–40 cm

Flowers: Lip convex, egg-shaped, 10–15 mm long, purplish-brown with a yellow margin, 2–12 in a loose spike; sepals purplish-pink

Leaves: Spear-shaped, pale green, the upper ones narrow

Fruits: Twisted, cylindrical capsule containing dust-like seeds

Lookalikes: Fly Orchid (*Ophrys insectifera*) has flowers 6–8 mm long, with a blackish-violet lip and green sepals, up to 14 per spike; it grows in woods, scrub and marshes.

Erect, short-lived perennial, arising from two egg-shaped tubers, of grassland and scrub on chalk and limestone, sand-dunes and low cliffs by the sea; it is erratic in appearance and may occur on quite new road-verges and cuttings. The flowers resemble a fat female insect and, although self-pollinated in the British Isles, are visited by males of a species of bee in S Europe. This plant is justifiably one of our most famous wild flowers and a great thrill to find, especially for the first time.

INDEX

Numbers in brackets indicate cross references in the text.